THE GREAT LIVES SERIES

Great Lives biographies shed an exciting new light on the many dynamic men and women whose actions, visions, and dedication to an ideal have influenced the course of history. Their ambitions, dreams, successes and failures, the controversies they faced and the obstacles they overcame are the true stories behind these distinguished world leaders, explorers, and great Americans.

Other biographies in the Great Lives Series

CHRISTOPHER COLUMBUS: The Intrepid Mariner

MIKHAIL GORBACHEV: The Soviet Innovator

ABRAHAM LINCOLN: The Freedom President

SALLY RIDE: Shooting for the Stars

HARRIET TUBMAN: Call to Freedom

ACKNOWLEDGMENT

A special thanks to educators Dr. Frank Moretti, Ph.D., Associate Headmaster of the Dalton School in New York City; Dr. Paul Mattingly, Ph.D., Professor of History at New York University; and Barbara Smith, M. S., Assistant Superintendent of the Los Angeles Unified School District, for their contributions to the Great Lives Series.

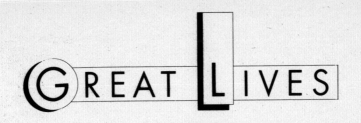

JOHN F. KENNEDY
COURAGE IN CRISIS

John W. Selfridge

FAWCETT COLUMBINE
NEW YORK

For middle school readers

A Fawcett Columbine Book
Published by Ballantine Books

Library of Congress Catalogue Card Number: 89-90826

ISBN: 0-449-90399-0

Cover design and illustration by Paul Davis

Manufactured in the United States of America

First Edition: September 1989

10 9 8 7 6 5 4 3 2 1

TABLE OF CONTENTS

1

Crisis in Cuba

A YEAR AND a half after he took office, President John Fitzgerald Kennedy was faced with one of the greatest challenges in the history of United States foreign policy. Surrounded by his able advisers in the White House situation room, the forty-five-year-old Kennedy pondered his next move. The tension was great; the stakes could not be higher. Never before had a United States president been in a situation in which an error in judgment or a failure to anticipate the thoughts and actions of an adversary could result in the instant destruction of entire countries. For the first time in history, nuclear war was a real possibility, and the fate of the world sat on one man's shoulders.

Since 1961, the United States had kept a watchful eye on Cuba, an island only ninety miles off the coast of Florida, suspecting that the Soviet Union was secretly planning to establish missile bases there.

When questioned about the possibility, Soviet leaders had repeatedly and angrily denied any such intention. Soviet Ambassador Anatoly Dobrynin had even stated publicly that the Soviet Union was interested above all in preserving the peace. He had insisted that the USSR (Union of Soviet Socialist Republics) was entirely aware of the hostile implications of placing nuclear missiles in the Western Hemisphere and had no intention of doing so.

But on October 15, 1962, only days after Dobrynin's public guarantees, McGeorge Bundy, special assistant for national security affairs, had shown President Kennedy incriminating aerial photographs of Cuba. The photographs revealed that a launching site for Soviet missiles was under construction approximately fifty miles southwest of Havana, Cuba's capital. American military experts had determined from the photos that missiles launched from such a site would most certainly hold nuclear warheads and could reach the American mainland in less than thirty minutes. Even worse, Soviet nuclear missiles in Cuba could threaten the military security of the entire Western Hemisphere.

President Kennedy called a meeting of the Executive Committee of the National Security Council (ExCom), a group consisting of the president's closest advisers from various governmental departments. The purpose of the meeting was to determine what course of action the United States would take in response to the Soviet Union's placement of missiles in Cuba.

President Kennedy and his advisers could not be sure from the start whether the Soviets had already delivered nuclear warheads to Cuba. Numerous aerial photography missions to Cuba were made, but the pictures did not prove anything definitively. If the Soviet warheads had already been delivered, the United States faced the prospect of nuclear war for any steps it might take. If no nuclear warheads had been delivered, the threat from the Soviets would be less dangerous.

Rather than alarm the American public, President Kennedy decided to keep what became known as the "Cuban Missile Crisis" a secret until more facts became available and until he and the Executive Committee had decided what measures to take. He and his advisers met in the evenings and often worked late into the night, discussing possible options, while by day they routinely performed the duties of their respective posts. Some nights Executive Committee advisers studied the crisis until dawn, taking only brief naps in their offices.

Eventually, the president decided to put his brother, Attorney General Robert F. Kennedy, in charge of the Executive Committee meetings. This way the president would not have to cancel appointments and thereby arouse the suspicion of the American public. During the crisis, the two Kennedy brothers, John and Robert, would become closer than they had ever been before.

On October 17, President Kennedy traveled to Connecticut, where he had a speaking engagement. He hoped that while he was gone the Executive

Committee, under the able direction of his brother, would devise a plan to resolve the crisis. But when the president returned to Washington, D.C., Robert greeted him at the airport with the news that the committee had not agreed on a plan. JFK was dismayed.

That evening the two brothers visited their father, Joe. Laughing and reminiscing with the elder Kennedy, John and Robert were able to gain strength from his company, just as they had done so many times before. They took comfort in easy conversation with their father; the problem of Soviet missiles in Cuba was not mentioned.

Some Executive Committee members recommended that the United States take immediate military action against Cuba. They argued that it was highly unlikely that the Soviet Union would strike back at the United States and become embroiled in a full-scale nuclear war over a tiny island in the Caribbean. Some members of Congress also urged a military attack. However, the president and his brother Robert believed moderation was the wisest course to follow under the circumstances. President Kennedy argued that the Soviets might indeed consider the island worth fighting over, given Cuba's unique strategic geographical location. Cuba under Soviet control could be used as a staging ground for exporting violent revolution to Mexico, Central and South America, and other countries in the Caribbean. Robert, however, emphasized that an attack launched by the United States against a small, underdeveloped, and considerably less powerful neighbor

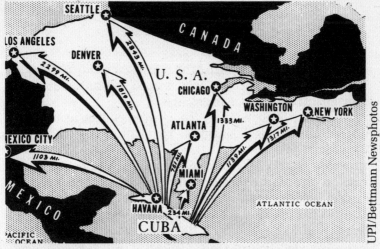

The Cuban Missile Crisis began after President Kennedy was informed that the Soviet Union had delivered nuclear missiles to Cuba. Above: This map shows the approximate distances from Cuba to key cities in the United States and Mexico. Below: President Kennedy with his cabinet and advisers at the White House during the crisis in October 1962. Risking war with the Soviets, Kennedy ordered a naval blockade of Cuba.

might not only fuel anti-Americanism in Latin America for years to come, but would probably not be supported by most Americans.

Adlai Stevenson, then the United States ambassador to the United Nations, recommended that the president propose that the Soviet Union remove its missiles from Cuba in exchange for the removal of United States missiles from Turkey, a country that shared borders with the Soviet Union and where the United States had housed missiles for years. President Kennedy decided that this course of action would not be appropriate, thinking that it would give the impression, both to the Soviets and to the world, that the United States had been frightened into a bargain.

President Kennedy and most of the Executive Committee members preferred the idea of a naval blockade. Kennedy pointed out that a fortress of American naval warships around Cuba could block any attempt to deliver weapons to the island and would send Soviet premier Nikita Khrushchev a message that the United States would not tolerate Soviet nuclear missiles in Cuba. Most important, such a blockade would give the Soviets an option to retreat, whereas a direct attack on Soviet missile bases might force the Soviets to retaliate against United States ships or cities. Still, as a precaution, Kennedy ordered the United States military to prepare for a possible invasion of Cuba. Tensions mounted and Executive Committee members struggled to decide their next move.

Though fully aware of the danger of his position, John Kennedy was steady under the strain as the crisis grew. Finally, after a thoughtful swim in the White House pool, where he spent an hour each day to relieve his back pain and to consider important matters in solitude, he decided to order American warships to surround Cuba.

At this point, the safety of his family became a particular concern for the president. He told his wife, Jackie, about the crisis and urged her to take their two children, Caroline and John, Jr., away from the nation's capital. Though he did not explain to her why he was suggesting they leave, she understood his concern. In the event of a nuclear war, Washington, D.C., and perhaps New York City would most likely be prime targets. With courage matching his, she decided to remain with her husband.

On October 22, 1962, only a week after the crisis had begun, the nation was stunned when President Kennedy announced on television that the United States faced the possibility of nuclear war with the Soviet Union. The American people were already aware that the United States was involved in an international conflict, but the actual details and the urgency of the crisis were not common knowledge.

From his White House office, the president revealed to millions of concerned Americans that the Soviets had placed nuclear missiles on the island of Cuba, and that these missiles, so close to the United States, posed a very serious threat to national security. President Kennedy made the American position very clear: The installation of nuclear missiles on

7

Cuba was a hostile Soviet act that could require drastic military action on the part of the United States — in other words, war!

Although at that time it had not been proven that nuclear warheads had actually been delivered to Cuba, aerial photographs showed that definite on-site preparations had been made for their delivery, that at least one missile was already there, and that thousands of Soviet military personnel were stationed on the island. President Kennedy's decision to blockade Cuba made the possibility of a direct conflict between the world's superpowers — the United States and the Soviet Union — more likely than at any other time in modern history. United States military forces all over the world were put on alert while 180 United States warships surrounded Cuba. Fighter planes were also sent into the area, in case a United States air strike became necessary. Now that it was public knowledge, congressional leaders and the media were kept up to date with each new development.

Not everyone felt the president's decision to blockade Cuba was the best one, but a poll showed that 84 percent of the American people agreed with the president's actions. Even those who argued in favor of other measures were glad John Kennedy was at the helm.

Robert Kennedy later said, "We went to bed that night filled with concern and trepidation, but filled also with a sense of pride in the strength . . . and the courage of the president of the United States."

Still, many Americans, believing that the Cuban Missile Crisis could escalate into a serious conflict between the superpowers or even into a third world war, prepared for the worst.

The actual dangers of the crisis were very uncertain. The Soviet ambassador continued to insist that there were no missiles in Cuba capable of hitting the United States. His claim had not been disproved by the aerial photos, since the one missile that had been spotted could have been used to defend Cuba rather than attack the United States. Still, the photos clearly showed that the construction of missile bases was well under way, so it was reasonable to suspect that Soviet ships sailing to Cuba might be carrying nuclear warheads to be aimed at American targets.

On the morning of the president's October 22 television address, the Executive Committee was informed that twenty-five Soviet ships and an undetermined number of submarines were headed for the United States naval blockade. But during the next few days, most of the ships retreated either before or immediately after entering the blockade zone. Some Soviet tankers and passenger ships were allowed through. United States military personnel boarded one ship, but nothing was found. Still, tensions continued to mount as the superpowers played cat-and-mouse in the Caribbean waters surrounding Cuba.

Finally, on Friday, October 26, Soviet diplomats made a proposal: The Soviet Union would remove its missiles if the United States would remove the blockade and vow not to invade Cuba. Soviet Premier

9

Khrushchev sent a cable to President Kennedy, in which he said: *We and you ought not now to pull on the ends of a rope in which you have tied the knot of war, because the more we pull, the tighter the knot will be tied. . . . Let us not only relax the forces pulling on the ends of the rope; let us take measures to untie that knot.*

However, for no apparent reason, Khrushchev suddenly changed his position. An ominous cable from the Soviet Premier followed, and a United States pilot flying over Cuba was shot down and killed. Just when there had appeared to be an end in sight, the crisis had taken a bad turn. Once again the dangerous situation in the Caribbean remained unresolved.

President Kennedy felt sure that Khrushchev wanted to avoid an escalation of the crisis. But Kennedy also suspected that the Soviet leader was under pressure from other high-ranking Soviet officials to consider a military solution, just as Kennedy himself had been urged by United States generals and certain Executive Committee members to attack Cuba. What United States action, Kennedy wondered, would make it possible for the Soviets to leave the Caribbean without looking as if they had been frightened away by a potential clash with American forces?

Robert Kennedy came up with an answer. His proposal was brilliant, yet simple: He suggested the president ignore Khrushchev's second message and respond only to the first. This tactic, Robert explained, would allow Khrushchev to pretend that he had forced the United States to make concessions — namely, to remove the blockade and to promise that there would be no invasion of Cuba. This could bring about a nonviolent resolution to the crisis. The president sent Khrushchev a message agreeing to the terms of the Soviet leader's first cable.

The following morning, on October 28, Khrushchev issued a statement saying the missiles would be dismantled, packed in crates, and returned to the Soviet Union. The world breathed a great sigh of relief.

2

To Be a Kennedy

THE STORY OF the Kennedys in America began in 1849, when John Kennedy's great-grandfather, Patrick Kennedy, boarded a ship in Ireland and set sail for the New World.

Throughout the early 1800s, poor Irish farmers and laborers left behind in Ireland what little they owned in the hope of making better lives for themselves in the United States and Canada. Then, in the 1840s, a devastating potato-crop failure in Ireland, in which more than one million people died of starvation or disease, caused the wave of Irish immigrants to the United States to rise considerably. Though many of those who attempted the difficult journey across the Atlantic never reached their destination, more than a million Irish immigrants were fortunate enough to reach the United States between 1846 and 1851. Patrick Kennedy, a young man from County Wexford, was one of them.

The vast majority of Irish immigrants who came to America did not feel fortunate at all, for they soon discovered that the horrible living conditions they had left behind were only slightly worse than those that lay ahead. Since these people had been poor farmers all their lives, back-breaking manual labor was the only way they knew to make a living. They moved into run-down apartment buildings, mainly in Boston, Massachusetts, and New York City, and looked for work. The luckiest found jobs that paid one dollar per day; others worked ten-or twelve-hour days for less, usually in factories that were dirty, overcrowded, and unsafe.

Poverty was not the immigrants' only burden. The poor treatment and hatred that the Irish encountered were worse than even the most skeptical immigrants had anticipated. As poor foreigners, the Irish immigrants had expected the usual difficulties experienced by people who sought entry into a society that considered them outsiders. They had not, however, expected their religion to prove an additional barrier. Though they were Catholics, whereas most Americans at the time were Protestants, they did not expect that difference to matter in a country that boasted "liberty and justice for all," and equality regardless of race, creed, or color.

For Patrick Kennedy, a poor, Irish Catholic immigrant, the chances of moving up America's social and economic ladder were slim. So when Patrick got a job in Boston as a dockhand, he never could have imagined that his great-grandson would one day become president. The work was hard, the pay low, and the boss a tyrant, but Patrick's courage and hard-working nature enabled him to get by. He married a young woman named Bridget Murphy, whom he had met on the ship from Ireland, and the couple went on to have three daughters and a son. Patrick learned how to make and repair wooden barrels and supported his family by working in East Boston, but the extremely hard life and unsanitary living conditions took their toll. Only nine years after his ship docked in Boston harbor, Patrick Kennedy died of cholera.

To support herself and her three children, Bridget Kennedy took a job as a clerk in a small Boston shop. Though her salary was very modest, eventually Bridget was able to buy the shop with money she had saved. Her son, Patrick Joseph, was also exceptionally thrifty and possessed a keen business sense. As he grew up, he saved his money, bought a saloon, and eventually ran his own liquor-importing business. Popular and respected in his community, Patrick Joseph entered politics and served three terms in the Massachusetts senate, paving the way for his future grandson, John F. Kennedy, to become interested in politics. Patrick married Mary Augusta Hickey, and in 1888 they had a son, Joseph Patrick, John Kennedy's father.

Joseph Patrick was slim with light, reddish-brown hair and piercing eyes. He was friendly and was an excellent student with an intense desire to succeed. He attended Harvard College, in Cambridge, Massachusetts, graduated in 1912, and immediately trained his eye on a career in banking. Like his father, Patrick, and his grandmother Bridget, Joseph had a talent for finances. Only a year after graduating from Harvard, Joseph Patrick Kennedy became one of the youngest bank presidents in the United States.

Joseph Patrick's success story was made even more complete in 1914 when he married Rose Fitzgerald, the daughter of John "Honey Fitz" Fitzgerald, a Boston politician and Massachusetts congressman. Rose was a short, slender woman with dark brown hair and green eyes. A devout Catholic, Rose had spent time teaching at a convent in Holland, and had also studied the piano. "I married for love," she later said, "but got money as a bonus."

The couple's first son, Joseph Patrick, Jr., was born a year later. John, whom the family often called Jack, was born on May 29, 1917. Their other children were Rosemary, Kathleen, Eunice, Patricia, Robert, Jean, and Edward.

Rose wanted her children to follow the Roman Catholic religion, so she had them study Church teachings, say their prayers every night, and go to mass every Sunday. Joe, Sr., a prominent Roman Catholic layman, often read aloud at Sunday mass.

Because Joe, Sr., was frequently away on business trips, Rose Kennedy was the one who raised and unified the young family. She was strict with her children and set firm household rules by which everyone was expected to abide. Those who broke the rules usually received a paddling.

The Kennedys instilled in all their children the same strong desire to succeed and sense of family loyalty that had been passed on from Kennedy to Kennedy since Joseph Patrick first set foot on American soil in 1849. Not unlike the Irish immigrants themselves, the close-knit Kennedy family had become a team, one that would settle for nothing short of victory. Indeed, "finish first" was the family motto. Later, in a *Time* magazine interview, President Kennedy looked back on his childhood: "Dad persuaded us to work hard at whatever we did. We soon learned that competition in the family was a kind of dry run for the world outside."

At fourteen, the Jack Kennedy enrolled at Choate, a competitive Connecticut preparatory school. Like so many boys and girls with older brothers and sisters, Jack frequently found himself in the shadow of his older brother, Joe, who also attended the distinguished New England boarding school. An excellent student and a fine athlete, Joe was his father's pride and joy.

Though Joe, Sr., loved all his children dearly, Jack, who received only average grades from his teachers, was somewhat less than his father's ideal. Sickly as a child, Jack was often in bed resting and reading stories, while other boys were attending classes or playing ball. These childhood illnesses would later give way to adult ailments that plagued Kennedy until his death. Jack's brother Bobby once said, "If a mosquito bit Jack, the mosquito would die."

Still, Jack was very strong-willed and determined to succeed despite these ailments. He constantly sought to measure up to his older brother in his

Kennedy at about the age of ten, while a student at the Dexter School in Brookline, Massachusetts. Almost all the Kennedy youths were sports enthusiasts who played hard to win. It is often said that this competitiveness trained them well for the rough and tumble of political life.

father's eyes — and in his own. So despite his poor health and frail build, Jack joined the Choate football team, just as his brother Joe had done. Like Joe, Jack was popular with his other classmates, who liked him for his wit and charm.

John Kennedy enrolled at Princeton University, in New Jersey, in 1935, making a clear break from the family tradition his father and older brother had started by going to Harvard. In fact, one of John's reasons for choosing Princeton was that he was now eighteen years old and tired of walking in his older brother's shadow. His health continued to hamper him, however, and he left the university before completing his first semester. John spent two months in a Boston hospital recovering from jaundice, and it took him the rest of the school year to regain his health.

The following fall the strength of family tradition won out, and John found himself at Harvard. Again determined to overcome his frailty and to compete successfully, John played football, hockey, rugby, and also joined the swim team. John surprised the Harvard coaches with his athletic ability, but he injured his back in football practice and was forced to quit the team.

That year, President Franklin Delano Roosevelt was running for reelection, and Joe, Sr., supported him. Roosevelt and the elder Kennedy were close, though intensely competitive, friends. One day, having heard that Joe, Sr., was interested in becoming ambassador to England, Roosevelt asked Kennedy to show him his legs. With a very puzzled look on his face, Kennedy respectfully complied with the president's request. Looking at Kennedy's bony, bowed legs, Roosevelt laughed and said, "Don't you know that the ambassador to the Court of St. James has to go through an induction ceremony in which he wears knee breeches and silk stockings? When photos of our new ambassador appear all over the world, we'll be a laughingstock!"

But in 1937 Roosevelt offered Kennedy the United States ambassadorship to Great Britain anyway. The association of Joe, Sr., with the Roosevelt administration exposed his son John to its liberal New Deal policies, which offered generous benefits and opportunities to all Americans. Family dinner conversation often focused on political topics, and the successes and failures of President Roosevelt's administration were frequently discussed in the Kennedy home during the 1930s and 1940s. Much of the liberalism that became a Kennedy tradition can thus be traced to Roosevelt's influence on Joe, Sr., and all the Kennedy children.

The ambassadorship to Great Britain was an especially important post in 1937 because at that time Europe stood on the brink of war. With his father in England, John, then twenty years old, became increasingly interested in European history and political affairs. He was intrigued by the way countries played the game of power politics, always trying to gain advantage over their neighbors. John began to study more and more European history at Harvard, and, with his brother Joe and sister Kathleen, he visited his father in Lon-

19

don. Europe was about to become a battleground, and the war there became a new focus for John's inquisitive mind.

3

World War II Hero

THE YEAR JOHN Kennedy celebrated his twenty-first birthday was not a happy one for most Europeans. The hardship of World War I was still fresh in their memories, and a new, perhaps greater threat loomed on the horizon. Watching the ominous events in Europe unfold during the late 1930s was, for Kennedy, like watching a frightening movie come to life.

The loss of World War I just more than two decades earlier had devastated Germany both politically and economically. The Treaty of Versailles, the official end of World War I, was signed in France on June 28, 1919. It stripped Germany of a considerable amount of territory, placed harsh restrictions on the German military, and forced Germany to pay large sums of money to other countries for war damages. The German government was left to rebuild its own cities, with little money available to complete the task. Massive unemployment resulted, goods became scarce, and the German economy hit rock bottom. Years of economic hardship ensued, and by the early 1930s the German people were ready to rebuild their country and eager for inspired leadership.

In the eyes of many Germans, Nazi party leader Adolf Hitler offered an opportunity to regain what had been lost in World War I. Hitler became Germany's chancellor, or leader, in 1933, and immediately set out to rearm the German military and set his sights on reclaiming the territory surrendered in Versailles.

By 1936, with the German people back to work and its economy gaining in strength, Hitler's evil plan to conquer the world was hatched. He formed a partnership with Italy, which was under the dictatorship of Benito Mussolini, and sent German forces into the Rhineland, the area west of Germany's Rhine River. This violation of the Treaty of Versailles marked Hitler's first attempt to expand Germany's borders.

Throughout 1938, Kennedy closely followed the newspaper accounts of Hitler's spreading power, as the German dictator ordered the occupation of Austria and quickly put Nazi policies into effect there. Hitler also wanted to recover the Sudetenland, a strip of land bordering Czechoslovakia.

In an attempt to appease Hitler's hunger for power and territory, France and Great Britain devised the Munich Pact. Under the terms of this agreement, Germany would be granted the Sudetenland in exchange for Hitler's promise not to invade Czechoslovakia. Hitler gladly accepted the terms of the pact, and, with the Sudetenland securely in his possession, he easily took control of neighboring Czechoslovakia.

John Kennedy looked on in disgust with the rest of the world as the German dictator conquered one piece of Europe after another. However, the United States remained uninvolved in European affairs, following an essentially isolationist foreign policy as Germany rapidly expanded. In September 1939, Germany invaded Poland.

One of Hitler's goals on the way to world domination was the annihilation of the Jews, a goal he had set years before he became chancellor. In a 1922 letter to a friend, Hitler wrote:

If I am ever really in power, the destruction of the Jews will be my first and most important job. . . . I will have gallows erected. . . . Then the Jews will be hanged, and they will stay hanging until they stink.

The Nazis convinced many of the German people, who badly wanted a scapegoat for their problems, that Jewish immigrants were responsible for Germany's economic ills after World War I. The Nuremberg Laws of 1935 furthered Hitler's anti-Semitic policies by denying Jews the right to vote and making it illegal for Germans to marry Jews or to do business with them.

On November 7, 1938, a young German Jew shot a German diplomat in Paris to protest Hitler's anti-Semitic policies. Two days later, the Nazis responded with a campaign of terror. The night of November 9 became known as Kristallnacht, or *The Night of the Broken Glass,* because of the countless pieces of shattered glass that flew through the air that evening. All across Germany, Jewish homes, businesses, and synagogues were burned, bombed, and looted. Approximately 20,000 Jews were arrested and sent to concentration camps, marking the beginning of Hitler's systematic effort to annihilate the Jews.

During this turbulent period, Kennedy, now in his final year at Harvard, traveled throughout Europe doing research for his senior thesis on the Munich Pact. The journey made a deep impression on him. He spoke to many Europeans, who told him of their fears and frustrations. Hitler's Nazism hung over free Europe like a dark cloud, and many Europeans welcomed the chance to express their concern. Being in Europe during this period gave Kennedy a perspective few Americans had at the time and was an experience he never forgot.

When his thesis was finished and presented to the faculty committee, it was praised highly, and in 1940 Kennedy graduated from Harvard College with honors. Joseph Kennedy, Sr., always eager to use his influence to help his sons, contacted some of his friends in the publishing industry and proposed that the thesis be made into a book. He circulated the manuscript, and an edited version was eventually published under the title *Why England Slept.* When the book later became a best-seller, the elder Kennedy beamed with pride, ignoring the fact that the book was extremely critical of British prime minister

Neville Chamberlain, whose policies Joe, Sr., had supported during the drafting of the Munich Pact. In 1940, when Winston Churchill replaced Chamberlain as England's prime minister, Joseph P. Kennedy's ambassadorship came to an end. He was summoned back to the United States because of his close association with the Chamberlain government, and a new ambassador was appointed.

As early as 1932, Churchill, then a member of British Parliament, had spoken and written about the Hitler menace. Now his worst fears were coming true. In 1940, Hitler invaded Norway, Denmark, Belgium, Luxembourg, the Netherlands, and France. The following year Germany invaded the Soviet Union, and within six months more than 600,000 Russian and Romanian Jews were murdered in the occupied Soviet territories. All of Europe was at war, and most people, including John Kennedy, were anticipating that the United States would soon be involved.

By this time a Kennedy tradition for military service was in the making. John's older brother, Joe, Jr., had been accepted as a naval cadet. Eager to follow in his brother's footsteps and serve his country, John tried to enlist, but because of his poor health he was turned down by both the navy and the army. Eventually his health improved, thanks to a summer of back-strengthening exercises, and his father made a few phone calls to the right people. John enlisted in the United States Navy in September 1941. His younger brother Bobby would do the same in 1943.

Japan, which had formally sided with Hitler and Mussolini on September 27, 1940, attacked the American military base at Pearl Harbor, Hawaii, on December 7, 1941. More than 2,400 American died in the swift but devastating attack, which lasted less than two hours. Four days later Hitler declared war on the United States, and on December 14 John Kennedy and millions of other Americans tuned in their radios to hear President Roosevelt declare war on Germany and Italy. The United States had officially entered World War II.

Kennedy completed a naval-officer training course and was assigned to a desk job at the Office of Naval Intelligence in Washington, D.C. For the most part, he found his new job dull and frustrating. He was soon transferred to Charleston, South Carolina, where he instructed defense-plant workers on how to protect their plants and themselves in the event of an enemy attack.

Like most young American men during World War II, John was eager to serve his country in battle. Once again his father's influence helped — John received a commission for sea duty. In July 1942, at the age of twenty-five, he enrolled at the Midshipmen's school at Northwestern University, in Illinois. At the earliest opportunity he volunteered for duty on a patrol torpedo (PT) boat. In 1943 John took command of PT 109, in the South Pacific.

In August 1943, PT 109 and thirteen other PT boats were sent to intercept a convoy of Japanese ships that was expected to travel in the vicinity of the Solomon Islands, in the South Pacific Ocean. Unable to locate the Japanese vessels, the disappointed crewmen of PT 109 began to return to their base on the island of Tulagi. Then, in a flash, the boat was blasted out of the water by a torpedo from a Japanese destroyer that had surprised the unsuspecting American crew. Two PT 109 crew members were killed in the attack.

With their boat in flames and sinking fast, the ten surviving crewmen were forced to swim for their lives. They looked back at the burning wreckage and knew the only chance they had was to stick together and to swim in search of land, at least a small island, where they could rest, tend to their wounds, and consider their next move.

With an injured crewman tied to him, Kennedy swam the lead, inspiring the others with his bravery and strength. He and his men swam nearly five miles before they finally reached land. That night, and again the next day, Kennedy left the island and swam to more frequently traveled waters in the hope of being spotted by a passing American boat, but his efforts were in vain. Tired and frustrated, the crewmen were about to give up, but Kennedy urged them on. The survivors then swam to another island, where they believed they would be more visible to American boats on patrol, and again Kennedy towed the injured man. Still, there was no sign of an end to their ordeal. Exhausted, hungry, and with little hope left, Kennedy and another sailor swam to a third island, called Nauro Island, where they met two natives with a canoe. Kennedy carved a short message into a coconut shell, and the islanders agreed to carry it forty miles to Rendova Harbor. Days later Kennedy and his surviving crew members were rescued.

Because of the courage he displayed in the South Pacific, Kennedy was awarded the Navy and Marine Corps Medal. The story of his heroism in the line of duty made the headlines of major United States newspapers. He was the subject of an article in *The New Yorker* magazine, and the rescue was recounted in several best-selling books. Suddenly, despite his modesty and his efforts to downplay the entire affair, John Kennedy had become a war hero. Ironically, the PT 109 incident had put such great strain on his back that he was forced to give up his command and return to the United States for medical treatment.

Meanwhile, the war raged on. By 1944 fighting had spread to all corners of the globe. The Allies, composed of the United States, Great Britain, and the Soviet Union, had made great strides in their effort to contain the Axis powers of Germany, Italy, and Japan. The inspired leadership of two United States generals in particular — Dwight David Eisenhower in Europe, and Douglas MacArthur in the South Pacific — was slowly bringing an end to the long, bitter war.

The most important breakthrough for the Allies was their June 6, 1944, invasion of the beachhead at Normandy, France, and the liberation of Paris from German occupation the following August. But there would be a lot more bloodshed before World War II would come to an end.

On August 12, 1944, John's older brother, Joseph, a United States Navy pilot stationed in England, embarked on a dangerous bombing mission. Tragically, only twenty-eight minutes after takeoff his plane exploded. The young Joe Kennedy, whom John so greatly admired, and for whom everyone had such high hopes, was dead.

The death of Joe, Jr., traumatized the entire Kennedy family, but his father was especially shaken. He had made so many grand plans for Joe, whom he had molded in his own image, instilling in him an intense desire for success in both business and politics that was much like his own. The ambassador had even suggested more than once that Joe might grow up to be president of the United States. Little did he know that his son John would be the Kennedy to achieve his country's highest office.

On April 12, 1945, President Roosevelt died and Harry S. Truman became the thirty-third president. In May 1945, Germany formally surrendered and the war in Europe was over. Fighting continued in the Pacific, but the United States was gaining decisive victories against Japan. One of those victories was the battle at Okinawa, which was fought in June and set the stage for the final United States assault on Japan.

United States forces had been bombing Japan since 1943, but in 1945 the bombing was intensified dramatically. In July alone, 42,000 tons of explosives were dropped on Japanese cities. Japan's economy was in a shambles and its people were resigned to defeat. Peace negotiations, held in Potsdam, Germany, were under way, but progress was slow. The United States, Great Britain, and China outlined terms for Japan's surrender, but Japan rejected the ultimatums.

In the meantime the United States government tested the first atomic bomb near Alamogordo, New Mexico, on July 16, 1945. Rather than allow the fighting to continue, increasing what had already been a great cost in human lives, President Harry S. Truman decided to use two atomic bombs on Japan to force that nation into surrendering immediately. On August 6, 1945, an American B-29 fighter plane dropped an atomic bomb on Hiroshima, Japan.

The force of the bomb was far greater than President Truman or American scientists had expected. More than half of the city's population of 320,000 was killed or maimed, and 62,000 homes were destroyed. Three days later, United States forces dropped another atomic bomb on the city of Nagasaki, killing more than 40,000 people and injuring many more. The world was shocked by the awesome power of the atomic bomb. Never before had human beings caused or witnessed such destruction. Now in shambles, Japan surrendered. World War II was finally over.

President Truman's decision to drop the atomic bomb on Japan has been both praised and criticized. Not only did the bomb destroy hundreds of thousands of lives in mere minutes, but the effects of radiation exposure on the Japanese population would be felt for decades to come.

Truman's decision also ushered in a brand-new period in history — the atomic age — in which the leaders of nations would have within their capacity the power to destroy cities and even entire countries in a given day. In America, those who would hold that power in their hands would be part of a new generation of leadership, and John Kennedy would be foremost among them.

4

Kennedy's Political Beginnings

IN IMPORTANT WAYS, John Kennedy was perfectly cut out for public life. He was handsome, he was from a well-known, affluent family with powerful connections, and he was a war hero. Joe, Sr., though he often said that John was too quiet and scholarly for politics, and especially Boston politics, repeatedly urged his son to give politics a try. After working briefly as a journalist, John Kennedy announced in 1946 that he would run for a seat in the United States House of Representatives.

Kennedy hoped to represent Boston's eleventh congressional district. Having known generations of Kennedys, citizens of the district's Irish and Italian working-class neighborhoods liked the young Democrat, even though Kennedy himself had spent most of his childhood in New York and on the Cape Cod seashore in Massachusetts. To them, John Kennedy represented a refreshing new style of politician. He was bright, energetic, recently back from gallantly serving his country overseas, and seemed to embody hope and to possess a vision for change.

Joseph Kennedy, Sr., very much at home in the world of power politics, jumped at the opportunity to help his son move up the political ladder. Though he generally stayed behind the scenes, Joe, Sr., supplied both moral and financial support to the campaign. He made phone calls to his various business associates, urging them to do their part to foster enthusiasm for and make contributions to John's candidacy.

In fact, all the Kennedys were eager to do whatever they could to help John's campaign. The women in the Kennedy family, when not going door to door handing out campaign buttons and brochures, were organizing afternoon tea parties for the district's women voters. A Kennedy tea was a social event not to be missed. Engraved invitations were sent out, and more than 1,000 women, a good many of them young women who were eager to shake John's hand, attended the first tea, which was held at the Hotel Commander in Cambridge, Massachusetts.

Despite young Kennedy's good looks and charm, and his family's endless enthusiasm, he was far from comfortable at the campaign podium. Always modest about his achievements, he seemed a bit uneasy when it came to speaking before crowds of people about his own unique abilities and why the public should vote for him. Still, he campaigned with unflagging energy. He spoke at apartment buildings, grocery stores, police stations, firehouses, taverns, barbershops, and beauty parlors, and the voters listened closely to what he had to say.

The people of the eleventh district were surprised that a young man from such a privileged background could have a real understanding of working-class problems. Even those from the district's poorest neighborhoods sensed that John Kennedy was on their side, eager to do whatever he could to help them improve their living conditions. His modesty, sincerity, and grace won them over. He picked up considerable support at every campaign stop, and on November 5, 1946, at the tender age of twenty-nine, he won the election by a landslide.

Congressman John Kennedy moved to Washington, D.C., on January 3, 1947, and immediately staked out his own territory in the House of Representatives. Though John was a liberal Democrat, he was somewhat conservative on foreign policy issues. Kennedy spoke out against President Truman's policy toward China and blamed his administration when China turned to communism. Kennedy criticized several of the administration's recent trade agreements and its spending priorities.

On domestic issues, Kennedy was decidedly liberal; he was for the disadvantaged and working class. He served on the Education and Labor Committee, defended organized labor, and kept one of his campaign promises by backing a veterans' housing bill. He supported rent and price controls, standing up to a powerful real estate lobby and its wealthy conservative allies in the House of Representatives. The junior congressman quickly earned a reputation as a maverick because he defied the usual liberal and conservative labels. He was an independent thinker who was willing to stand his ground and speak his mind on the House floor, no matter who disagreed with him.

In 1947, Kennedy traveled to Europe on a fact-finding mission. After a brief stop in Ireland to visit his sister Kathleen, he went on to London, where he became seriously ill. Kennedy returned to the United States by ship, receiving intensive medical care during the entire ocean voyage. Though medication helped to improve his condition, doctors feared that he had only a few more years to live. Even Kennedy sensed that his chances for full recovery were very slim, but he refused to give up without a fight.

To everyone's surprise, John recuperated from his illness and resumed his active social life. He went out regularly with friends and dated a number of young women. Still, he never developed a serious relationship with any of his girlfriends, perhaps because he expected to live only a few more years.

On May 12, 1948, the Kennedys received word that Kathleen, or "Kick," as the family called her, and a friend had been killed in a plane crash in England. Kathleen was John's favorite sister. He recovered slowly from the loss, but when he finally did bounce back completely he did so with a renewed passion for living. Having lost his brother Joe, then his sister Kathleen, and being seriously ill himself, John was determined to live every day he had left to the fullest.

John Kennedy, now thirty-one years old, ran un-
opposed in the 1948 election. He was reelected for a
third term in 1950, but he found himself increasingly bored by his work in the House. In fact, during his
very first year in the nation's capital, Kennedy had
realized that the House of Representatives did not
offer enough challenges to satisfy his ambitions. He
had a strong desire to become more involved in foreign affairs. Despite his poor health and his sometimes debilitating back problem, John decided to
run for the United States Senate.

In the fall of 1951, John, his sister Pat, and his
brother Bobby traveled to Israel and the Far East.
John was profoundly affected by what he saw in
Southeast Asia, especially in Vietnam. For more
than seventy years, the people of Vietnam had been
under French colonial rule, and, in recent decades,
their struggle for independence had greatly intensified. Vietnam also suffered from internal struggles,
as various Vietnamese groups tried to gain political
power in the process of ousting the French. Kennedy
was shocked to witness how decades of war had
divided and shattered this tiny country.

While traveling together the three Kennedys
learned a great deal about one another. During the
trip the two brothers, eight years apart in age, became friends. Because of their age difference, John
and Bobby had not really grown up together, so in a
way they were getting to know each other for the
first time. It was the beginning of a very close relationship, one that would mean a great deal to them

for the rest of their lives, and one that would even make history.

While in Japan, John once again became ill and was forced to return home, but the trip had awakened something in him. When he recovered, he spoke frequently of the urgent need for the United States to help the world's poorer countries.

John Kennedy, only thirty-three years old, began his campaign for the United States Senate in the spring of 1952. His Republican opponent, Henry Cabot Lodge, had served twelve years in the Senate, came from an established Massachusetts family, and had many strong, influential supporters in the state. To defeat Lodge would require hard work and efficient organization. John asked his brother Bobby to run the campaign.

Kennedy's father, Joe, Sr., had wanted to run his son's campaign, but his style of politics and some of his political beliefs were old-fashioned and clashed with John's "new generation" image. When Bobby was named campaign manager, the elder Kennedy was content to work behind the scenes, as he had done so diligently for John in the past. Joe, Sr., made numerous phone calls, some of which would have met with John's disapproval had he known about them, and he also helped out financially. Lodge was a tough opponent, but he made some crucial mistakes in his campaign. One of those mistakes was to underestimate the Kennedy campaign, particularly Bobby's abilities as a campaign manager. Another was to agree to a debate with John Kennedy that October. In the debate, sponsored by the League of

Women Voters, John Kennedy proved to be quicker, smarter, and more confident than Lodge. Not only was Kennedy more comfortable than his opponent when it came to discussing the issues, but he was courteous and good-natured, traits rarely displayed in the politics of the time. Kennedy charmed the audience with his wit and warmth; it seemed he could have won the debate easily on personality alone. This was the graceful and intelligent Kennedy that most Americans would come to know and, in many cases, idolize.

Still, even after the debate many experts considered Lodge the favorite, expecting him to win reelection — if not on his own popularity then on the prestige of the heavily favored Republican presidential candidate that year, Dwight Eisenhower. It was thought that the majority of people who supported President Eisenhower would also vote for his fellow Republican in the coming election. When the votes were counted, however, the Kennedy camp rejoiced — John had won the election with 51 percent.

While making his bid for the Senate, Kennedy had also been busy trying to win the affections of a young woman named Jacqueline Bouvier, whom he had met at a dinner party in 1951 while she was a student at Georgetown University, in Washington, D.C. Though Kennedy later described their meeting by saying, "I leaned across the asparagus and asked her for a date," Jacqueline denied there being any asparagus on the table. Jackie, as she was called, had spent a year at Vassar College, then studied at the Sorbonne in France. Now she was working as a reporter at the *Washington Times-Herald*, where John's sister Kathleen had once worked.

Like John, Jackie came from an affluent family, was very well-educated, and was quite popular among Washington socialites. A slim brunette with large brown eyes and a pleasant smile, she was fluent in French and German, she loved to ride horses, and was passionate about art, literature, and music. Though twelve years younger than John, Jackie was poised, though soft-spoken, and private in her thoughts and feelings. Still, she never hesitated to speak her mind, and she was often very determined and even stubborn when it came to getting her way. Her stepsister, Nina Straight, said of Jackie, "She has guts, taste, and style." John was intrigued by Jackie the moment he met her, and she was attracted to him as well.

John Kennedy made the transition from the House of Representatives to the Senate quite naturally. As he had done in the House, Kennedy quickly asserted his independence, often arguing against the policies of the Eisenhower administration. He was particularly opposed to the administration's request for $400 million in military assistance for France, which was fighting a war to prevent Vietnam's independence. Since his trip to Southeast Asia, Kennedy had his own opinions on what role the United States should play in that part of the world.

Vietnam had been under French rule since the 1850s, and for decades nationalist and Communist rebels had been at war with the French colonial government. Kennedy argued that a substantial portion of any United States money sent to Vietnam should go for nonmilitary aid to the Vietnamese people, who were devastated by years of war. He objected to fueling the French military effort there primarily because he did not believe the French could score a military victory in the jungles of Vietnam. Ironically, Kennedy would later lead the United States into making some of the same mistakes as the French in Vietnam.

In the Senate, Kennedy also criticized the Eisenhower administration's efforts to cut the defense budget. A conservative on the issue of military spending, Kennedy argued that reducing the defense budget would hamper United States influence around the globe and would make the United States dangerously vulnerable to foreign and especially Soviet aggression.

John continued to see Jackie regularly. Joe, Sr., not only approved of Jackie, but he liked her very much. In an effort to encourage his son's interest in her, the elder Kennedy tried to impress upon John the importance of a good wife to a political career. In the spring of 1953, in a trans-Atlantic phone call, John asked Jackie to marry him. She accepted his proposal.

Though she continued to find Joe, Sr., charming, Jackie did not get along easily with the other Kennedys. Her ways were very different from theirs. The Kennedys were robust, while Jackie was delicate and quiet. They were competitors who enjoyed sports such as sailing, tennis, and touch football. Jackie preferred to spend her time painting, reading, or taking walks. Jackie, who once broke an ankle playing touch football on the lawn at the Kennedy summer home in Hyannis Port, on the southern coast of Massachusetts, nicknamed the Kennedy sisters "the rah-rah girls." On a picnic, the Kennedys would bring sandwiches, apples or peaches, maybe some chocolate chip cookies, and milk or fruit juice, whereas Jackie would bring imported cheeses, French bread, some exotic fruit, maybe a wedge of quiche, and wine or mineral water. Jackie once said, "I'm not going to be what they want me to be . . . I won't cut my hair. I won't go out and talk. I won't have twenty-five kids."

When John Kennedy was thirty-six years old he married Jacqueline Bouvier. Their wedding, on September 23, 1953, was one of the most celebrated national social events of the year. When it came to building a life together, however, they often had different interests. John often put his work first, and as a result Jackie sometimes felt neglected.

Meanwhile, the Soviet Union, then the world's most powerful Communist state, and the United States were in a state of disharmony. The two countries had emerged from World War II as superpowers. But instead of cooperation between the former allies, a period of mutual distrust had ensued, an era which came to be called the Cold War. In the United States the Cold War period was characterized by a deeply rooted fear of communism, at home as well as abroad. Communism, as practiced in the Soviet Union, was a totalitarian form of government. The state owned all goods and means of producing goods. Many Americans were afraid that communism might spread to the United States and undermine traditional American values such as freedom of speech, freedom of religion, and free enterprise.

The House of Representatives Un-American Activities Committee was a group public officials who sought to expose Communists within the United States government, and people everywhere suspected others of being Communist sympathizers. This fear was compounded by the Communist movements in China, Korea, Indochina, and the Philippines, as well as by the Soviet domination of Eastern Europe.

More than anyone else during the early 1950s, Senator Joseph McCarthy of Wisconsin fueled the fears and anxieties of an alarmed, anti-Communist American public. He used the prevailing wave of anti-Communist feelings for his own political gain, playing on those fears under the guise of public service. McCarthy made many irresponsible and entirely undocumented charges against people in government, entertainment, and the media, very often destroying lives and careers. For a time, anyone Senator McCarthy accused of being a Communist or of having past or present associations with Communists was under great pressure to prove his or her innocence, or else be blacklisted. Once blacklisted, an individual found it impossible to get work.

Rabid anticommunism swept the nation. The government distributed pamphlets, such as "One Hundred Things You Should Know About Communism," fostering suspicion and urging people to inform on their friends and neighbors. The media created a state of paranoia and hysteria. Major magazines ran articles with titles such as "Communists Are After Your Child" and "How Communists Get That Way." Movies such as *I Married a Communist* played at local theaters everywhere; more than forty such films were released between 1948 and 1954. Books discussing the merits of communism were banned. The suppression of one such book perhaps best illustrates the frenzy that characterized the times — *The Selected Works of Thomas Jefferson*, edited by Philip Foner.

Senator Joe McCarthy had known the Kennedys for a long time. He and John had been freshmen representatives together, and McCarthy had visited the Kennedy house at Hyannis Port, especially while he was dating John's sister Pat. Joe, Sr., supported McCarthy, and John also had been a staunch anti-Communist as a member of the House. Bobby Kennedy even worked on the McCarthy Committee for six months.

As "McCarthyism" continued to divide the nation, however, John Kennedy sought to distance himself from its chief spokesman. In March 1954, McCarthy accused certain high-ranking United States Army personnel of having Communist sympathies. President Eisenhower, never a supporter of McCarthy, and especially revolted by his tactics, issued statements denouncing him and his associates as irresponsible troublemakers. Eisenhower also blocked McCarthy's requests for access to FBI files, which the senator claimed he needed in order to prove his theory that the army had been infiltrated by Communists and Communist sympathizers.

An official measure to condemn Senator McCarthy was presented in the Senate in October 1954. This put the Kennedys in a very awkward situation. Joe, Sr. continued to support McCarthy, but John did not, even though he had not publicly criticized him. Senator Kennedy knew he would have to think long and hard before casting his vote for or against McCarthy in December.

In October, Kennedy's back problem was causing him so much pain that he entered the hospital to undergo surgery to fuse two disks in his back. Bobby Kennedy once said of his brother John, "At least half the days that he spent on this earth were days of intense physical pain." Though the operation itself was a success, John contracted a staph infection and lapsed into a coma. His wife, Jackie, was by his side day and night. Eventually he recovered, and by Christmas he was ready to leave the hospital.

While Senator John Kennedy was in the hospital, the Senate condemned McCarthy by a vote of 67 to 22, putting an end to the McCarthy era. Kennedy never revealed how he would have voted had he been present. Most agree that it was one crisis situation he was glad he did not have to face.

John began a long period of recovery in Palm Beach, Florida. For Christmas he bought Jackie an easel, paints, and some brushes. Immobilized, John himself began painting, and this proved both enjoyable and therapeutic. He painted everything — people, still lifes, landscapes — and often worked from morning until late at night. Still, he never really acquired the knack. "He did a lot of terrible paintings, but he was enjoying himself," a friend recalled.

Jackie was extremely supportive as her husband's health improved, and the couple became closer during that period. She encouraged John to spend his many idle hours writing. He had been planning to write a book of character portraits of numerous political leaders who had taken unpopular stands regardless of the political consequences. His book, *Profiles in Courage,* would win the Pulitzer Prize for history in 1957.

After a second back operation, in 1955, John Kennedy was back in the Senate. Joe, Sr., made a phone call to Senate majority leader Lyndon Johnson and got John a post on the Senate Foreign Relations Committee. But at the age of thirty-eight, Kennedy had lost interest in the Senate. In 1956, friends and associates urged Kennedy to run for the vice-presidency with the likely Democratic nominee, Adlai Stevenson. At a dinner party several months prior to the National Democratic Convention that year, Stevenson adviser Bill Blair pleaded with Kennedy to consider the possibility. Jackie asked a *Newsweek* reporter at the party, "Why is Bill trying to persuade Jack to run for vice-president, when Jack really wants to be president?"

5

President Kennedy:
The New Frontiersman

IN 1956, AT the young age of thirty-nine, John
Kennedy was a well-known national leader.
Meanwhile, Democratic party delegates agreed
that Adlai Stevenson, a former governor of Illinois,
would receive the party's nomination for the presidency at the Democratic National Convention in August. Stevenson was considering three Democratic
senators for his running mate. John Kennedy was
one of them.

Kennedy had good reason to believe that he would
be selected by Stevenson to run with him as vice-
president. First, his reputation and support in the
Senate was solid. Second, Kennedy's conservative
stands on defense would strike an effective balance
with what many perceived to be Stevenson's overly
liberal views. But rather than making the choice

himself and possibly alienating supporters of the two hopefuls who were not chosen, Stevenson left the decision to the convention delegates. After three ballots, Tennessee Senator Estes Kefauver was selected as Stevenson's running mate.

Kennedy was extremely disappointed because it was his first political defeat. He called his father and said, "We did our best, Dad. I had fun and I didn't make a fool of myself." He did, however, enjoy some time in the spotlight when he delivered the convention's nominating speech.

Kennedy left for Europe. He had planned a trip to France with some friends after the convention, win or lose. Jackie, who was pregnant, did not want her husband to leave, but told him to go, knowing that a vacation would do him good. While John was on the Italian Riviera, Jackie had a miscarriage. He returned immediately to be by her side, but within days he was on the road again, campaigning for Adlai Stevenson across the United States.

Despite his losing the bid for vice-president, Kennedy had strengthened his national image in 1956. He had given an inspiring speech at the convention. He proved his loyalty to the Democratic party, campaigning hard for the Democratic nominee. Perhaps most important, when Stevenson lost the election to President Eisenhower that year, Kennedy had not gone down with the sinking ship. On the contrary, Kennedy's political future had never looked better. As a young girl wrote to Kennedy after his defeat: "I cried when you didn't win. Just wait till I'm a little older. I'll vote for you to be president." Stevenson himself said that Kennedy would be "the one person people will remember from the convention."

Stevenson was right. The convention had made Kennedy a rising star. Still, in a *Time* magazine interview soon after the convention, Kennedy said, "Nobody is going to hand me the nomination. When the time is ripe, I'll have to work for it." With his eye on the next presidential race, Kennedy campaigned hard during the following two years for reelection to the Senate. He gave more than 300 speeches across the nation, building his reputation as well as his confidence. In the 1958 senatorial race, Kennedy earned 73.6 percent of a record turnout. The decisive victory thrust him even further into the national spotlight and brought him almost automatic consideration for the Democratic presidential nomination in 1960.

One of Kennedy's favorite stories was about an Irishman who stood before a tall wall thinking how difficult it would be to climb over. The man then threw his hat over the wall so that there would be no question that he had to try. On January 2, 1960, John Kennedy officially announced that he intended to seek the Democratic party's nomination for the presidency of the United States; he had thrown his hat over the wall — and into the ring for the Democratic nomination for president.

John and Jackie bought a house in the Georgetown section of Washington, D.C. In November 1957 she gave birth to a daughter, Caroline, hired servants, and redecorated their new home. Her taste was superb, and in an important way she brought style and excellence to the household, a lot of which rubbed off on John, who became more interested in the arts and took much greater care with his appearance.

Though John Kennedy was making great strides in his political career, he had three major hurdles to overcome before he could secure his nomination: his age, his religion, and his conservative politics. If elected, Kennedy, at forty-three would be the youngest United States president in history, and some believed he needed more experience and maturity before he would be capable of holding office. He would also be the first Catholic to become president, and some voters feared that once in office Kennedy would have a greater loyalty to the Pope than to his country and its Constitution. Finally, many political experts believed that Kennedy was not liberal enough to appeal to the working-class voters who made up much of the Democratic party.

The issue of Kennedy's being a Catholic was the one that most threatened his campaign, and John skillfully put it to rest. "If a President breaks his oath," he said, "he is not only committing a crime against the Constitution, for which the Congress can impeach and should impeach him, but he is committing a sin against his God." Shrewdly conjuring up a sacred American ideal — that any youngster born in the United States, rich or poor, regardless of race or religion, could grow up to be president — Kennedy told voters, "If this election is decided on the basis that forty million Americans lost their chance of being president on the day they were baptized, then it is the whole nation that will be the loser in the eyes of history, and in the eyes of our own people."

John and Jackie traveled together on the long and arduous campaign trail. She disliked politics, but she wanted to be with her husband. She quickly got used to living out of a suitcase and learned to play the role of a candidate's wife — smiling, wearing elegant clothes, offending no one, and making friendly conversation with reporters. Jackie frequently gave short speeches at rallies, pointing up her husband's strengths but never discussing issues. John's brother Robert also made numerous public appearances. The Kennedy political machine seemed unstoppable.

The reward for all their hard work came in Los Angeles, California, at the Democratic National Convention in July 1960. John Kennedy won the party's nomination for president, with 806 delegate votes. His closest challenger, Texas Senator Lyndon Baines Johnson, got only 409 votes.

Across America thirty-five million people watched on their television sets as John Kennedy accepted the nomination. In his acceptance speech, Kennedy touched on the theme of "A New Frontier," an inspiring idea which would capture the imagination of the American people and carry John Kennedy to the White House:

. . . . We stand today on the edge of a New Frontier — the frontier of the 1960s — a frontier of unknown opportunities and perils — a frontier of unfulfilled hopes and threats . . .[and] the New Frontier of which I speak is not a set of promises — it is a set of challenges. It sums up not what I intend to offer the American people, but what I intend to ask of them. . . .

Though many advised him against it, Kennedy selected Lyndon Johnson as his running mate, and he did so for two main reasons. First, Johnson had served as Senate majority leader, and consequently had a great deal of influence in Congress. Any effective president needed friends in Congress. Second, Johnson was a Southerner, and the South would be an important battleground in the election in November. Kennedy hoped that Johnson's presence on the ticket would deliver the Southern vote for the Democrats.

The Republicans nominated Richard M. Nixon at the Republican National Convention on July 27 in Chicago, Illinois. Nixon had served as vice-president in the Eisenhower administration, and, because of Eisenhower's popularity, was ahead of Kennedy in the early polls. Also, Nixon had delivered an excellent acceptance speech at the Republican convention.

Still, many Americans were concerned that since World War II the Soviet Union had made greater strides in science and technology than the United States. Though most voters at that time supported Nixon, many were beginning to think that John Kennedy offered greater hope for change and advancement into the next decade.

Indeed, as the campaign season unfolded, many voters were slowly won over by the Kennedy charm and wit, especially when compared to Nixon's stiff, dull manner. Kennedy's easy rapport with the press was also an enormous advantage. One reporter recalled a story that illustrated the difference in the styles of the two candidates. A group of reporters traveled with each of the candidates during the campaign season. When some air turbulence caused the Nixon campaign jet to take a sudden, startling drop, Nixon staffers uneasily asked the reporters on the plane not to mention the incident in their news articles. When the Kennedy staff jet ran into similar difficulties, John joked with the reporters, "If we'd really gone down, I just want you fellows to know that your names would have been in very small type."

Kennedy was extremely popular with women voters, and this popularity was a tremendous asset to the campaign. In fact, there was a kind of Kennedy mania that was understood only by women. Teenage girls, married women with children, middle-aged women, and elderly women alike were taken by the Kennedy charm. At campaign rallies, many women screamed, cried, or shook uncontrollably. Bolder ones pushed through large, cheering crowds just to touch the candidate or get him to look at them, and many tried, often successfully, to take home a piece of his clothing as a souvenir. One reporter noted that in the aftermath of a typical Kennedy campaign rally there would be pairs of women's shoes in the streets, abandoned by women who had either discarded them in order to run after Kennedy's car or literally leaped out of them from sheer excitement.

The Nixon campaign was doing very well, particularly in the South and in the Midwest. Though Nixon had run into some difficulties, crowds were generally receptive to him across the country. The vice-president started campaigning early and continued to campaign aggressively during the early weeks of the season. The polls varied, as they usually do, but most experts agreed that through the middle of September, Vice-president Nixon had sustained his early lead and was likely to win the presidential race.

Perhaps the most decisive campaign events in 1960 were the televised debates between the two candidates. Today we take television campaign advertising and televised political debates for granted, but in 1960 the role of television in American politics had not yet been determined. Four debates were scheduled — September 26, October 7, October 13, and October 21 — each to be carried by one of the major television networks.

The Kennedy campaign staff did an excellent job of anticipating the themes and issues Nixon would raise in the debates and had prepared organized, detailed responses to questions they expected Nixon to ask. Kennedy thus came across as cool and confident under pressure, and very knowledgeable.

The most crucial feature of the debates, however, was how the candidates looked to the television audience. Nixon was haggard from campaigning. He had lost nearly ten pounds, and his skin was pale. Though he was given a shave minutes before the

Kennedy received a tumultuous welcome from Chicago
politicians and supporters as he arrived for the first of his
television debates with Vice-president Richard Nixon on
September 26, 1960. The debates are commonly believed to
have ushered in a new era in American politics in which
a candidate's television persona is crucial to success.

broadcast of the first debate, his makeup did not conceal the dark stubble on his face, and he perspired heavily under the hot studio lights. By contrast, Kennedy looked young, energetic, and calm. He was tanned and required only a little makeup, to dull the shine of the bright lights on his nose. His dark blue suit, unlike Nixon's light gray one, contrasted well with the light-colored studio backdrop. While the sensitive cameras picked up even the tiniest flaws in Nixon's appearance, Kennedy gave off a healthy, almost perfect glow. In the world of television, a tired-looking Nixon simply could not compete with the youthful, handsome John Kennedy. It is interesting to note that Nixon won the debate in polls taken of people who heard it only via radio. Yet, after the debates, Kennedy was suddenly the favorite, with polls indicating that he would win handily in the national election.

On November 8, 1960, John F. Kennedy became the thirty-fifth president-elect of the United States. He also became the first Catholic president and, at the age of forty-three, the youngest person to be elected to the nation's highest office. John Kennedy received 303 electoral votes to Richard Nixon's 219 in a record voter turnout. These figures, however, do not reveal how close the election actually was. Kennedy received only one-tenth of one percent more of the popular vote of the nearly 69,000,000 people who went to the polls than Nixon did, thus defeating his opponent by less than 120,000 votes.

In such close elections, the victor owes a great deal to his campaign staff and, particularly, to his campaign manager, for only shrewd planning, smart execution, and split-second decision making can turn a tight race into victory on Election Day. To this extent, Kennedy owed much to his brother Robert, who ran a brilliant presidential campaign, and who had become John's chief political adviser and most trusted confidant.

In the weeks leading up to his inauguration on January 20, 1961, Kennedy, in close consultation with Robert, put together a list of "the best and the brightest" people in Washington for possible cabinet posts, regardless of political affiliation. He selected Robert McNamara, a former head of the Ford Motor Company and a Republican, as secretary of defense. Two more Republicans were given the same positions they had held in the Eisenhower administration: Douglas Dillon was named secretary of the treasury, and Dean Rusk was named secretary of state. McGeorge Bundy, yet another Republican, was appointed special assistant for national security affairs, an important foreign-policy position.

Kennedy was criticized for appointing his brother Robert attorney general. Robert Kennedy, a University of Virginia Law School graduate, had never practiced law or tried a case and therefore was not considered qualified for such a high-level legal post. John disarmed the critics by joking, though only half seriously, that the appointment would be a good way for Bobby to get some experience.

Meanwhile, as John was on his way to the Kennedy Florida home late in November, he was regaled with news from Washington — "It's a boy!" Jackie, who had stayed behind in the capitol, had given birth to their second child, and first son, John Fitzgerald Kennedy, Jr.

On January 20, 1961, a bitterly cold, blustery day in Washington, D.C., Kennedy delivered one of the shortest inauguration speeches ever given by a United States president. However, the speech was not short on inspiration. Again Kennedy put forth the themes he had presented at the Democratic Convention, the same themes that had endeared him to millions of Americans along the campaign trail. He made it clear that the 1960s would be a decade of challenge, that only a concerted effort would realize America's hopes and dreams:

> Let every nation know . . . that we shall pay any price, bear any burden, meet any hardship, support any friend, oppose any foe, to assure the survival and success of liberty. . . . Let us never negotiate out of fear. But let us never fear to negotiate. . . . All this will not be finished in the first one hundred days. Nor will it be finished in the first one thousand days, nor in the life of this administration, nor even perhaps in our lifetime on this planet. But let us begin.

Finally, he issued a challenge that would ring in the ears of generations after him: "And so, my fellow Americans, ask not what your country can do for you — ask what you can do for your country."

6

The Cold Warrior

WHEN THE KENNEDYS moved into the White House in January 1961, Jackie observed that it was more like an office building than a home. The walls were painted a very official-looking pale green. The large windows were covered by thick, heavy shades, the kind with ropes and pulleys that one usually found in a courthouse, town hall, public school, or library. President Eisenhower had taken all his personal belongings with him, leaving empty walls, tables, desks, and shelves. The sooty fireplaces had not been used in years and needed a thorough cleaning before they could be used to warm the many rooms of the presidential mansion. Jackie wondered if her family could ever be comfortable living in such a stark, impersonal environment.

Before long, the First Lady employed her excellent taste and turned the White House into a home. She hired decorators to help. In the basement she found an old desk. It had been presented to President Rutherford B. Hayes in 1878 by Queen Victoria of England, and was later used by President Franklin D. Roosevelt during his famous Fireside Chat radio broadcasts. Jackie had the dull, tired desk sanded, refinished, and moved into her husband's office, much to his satisfaction. In a short time she made the White House a warm and welcoming place for guests. The president decorated his office with family photographs, sports memorabilia, and Navy souvenirs, including the coconut shell from Nauro Island.

In restoring the White House, the new First Lady paid close attention to every detail. She used the mansion's history as her guide, filling the house with appropriate Early American furnishings. Later her efforts motivated Congress to declare the White House a national monument, and in 1962 she arranged for the publication of *The White House Guide Book*.

With the Kennedys in the White House, it was the first time since President Theodore Roosevelt's terms, 1901 to 1909, that it served as a home for young children. Caroline played in the Oval Office, and John-John would run merrily across the White House lawn.

The atmosphere in the White House during the Eisenhower administration was very formal. Perhaps this was because President Eisenhower had once been General Eisenhower, a West Point graduate and a career military man. Kennedy's style was

President Kennedy and his wife Jacqueline arrive at a Washington reception after the inaugural ceremonies on January 20, 1961. The Kennedys were the youngest "first couple" in history. They made the White House into a real home—it had been many years since little children had lived there—and into a center for American culture as well.

very much the opposite. For example, one night, just as President Kennedy was about to go to bed, he noticed a Secret Service agent standing guard outside the front door of the White House. It being an especially cold night in February, he asked the man to come inside to get warm. The agent politely declined, saying that he was on duty and that he was under orders to stay outside. Kennedy went upstairs and put on a coat. He returned carrying a second coat for the guard and two cups of hot chocolate, which they drank together, chatting on the frozen White House steps. President Kennedy treated his Cabinet and other close advisers like members of his family, and they, in turn, were extremely loyal to him. He encouraged dialogue, and he constantly discussed important matters with his advisers. Kennedy often had brainstorming sessions with his staff, in which he would ask each adviser to present a view on a particular issue. Kennedy would make the final decision only after hearing all their opinions and weighing the merits of each. Men such as Kenny O'Donnel, Larry O'Brian, Pierre Salinger, and Ted Sorensen formed a collection of friends, political operators, and wordsmiths who were dedicated to Kennedy and captivated by his powerful charisma.

Kennedy was always very well prepared for these brainstorming sessions. A speed reader of more than 1000 words per minute, Kennedy quickly absorbed the contents of newspapers, magazines, and books, as well as the reams of memoranda and reports his advisers prepared for him. He was able to recall with extraordinary accuracy the smallest of details, even citing page numbers on occasion.

During the first three months of his administration, Kennedy gave ten press conferences, including the first prescheduled televised press conference ever given by a president. Kennedy was a natural in front of television cameras. At these televised press conferences, he glowed with confidence and displayed an exceptional ability to answer questions spontaneously in an organized, intelligent fashion. Kennedy was the first television president, and America loved what it was seeing and hearing. His manner, alternately serious and witty, reassured the American people that the country was in competent hands, and watching the president in action right in their own living rooms thrilled them.

Jackie Kennedy continued to bring refinement and taste to the White House. While she and her husband were dating, Jackie had introduced him to classical music. As First Lady, she brought musicians to the White House and organized chamber-music concerts both inside the mansion and on the lawn. American violinist Isaac Stern and Russian-born pianist Vladimir Horowitz, two of the world's greatest musicians, played for the Kennedys. Nobel Prize winners and famous artists were also guests of the First Family. America took a great deal of pride in the new administration, which seemed unlike any that had preceded it.

The Kennedys were young, well mannered, extremely intelligent, and highly cultured. When it came to staff appointments, the Kennedys surrounded themselves with other brilliant idealists who were eager to change the world. In 1960, anything seemed possible. This optimism was central to Kennedy's popularity and success.

The Kennedy team members certainly had their work cut out for them. They had inherited serious problems abroad, including the Cold War with the Soviet Union and the spread of communism to Latin America, Europe, and Southeast Asia. On January 30, 1961, President Kennedy delivered his first State of the Union address. He presented an overview of the problems facing the nation both at home and abroad, and he proposed solutions to those problems.

During his State of the Union address, President Kennedy said, "We must show the world what a free economy can do." He announced the formation of the Food for Peace program, which would deliver surplus American food to needy countries abroad. He saw the program as having two purposes, one obvious and the other subtle. Of course, the main purpose of the program was to help fight world hunger, but Kennedy also hoped that America's effort to feed the hungry would indirectly counter the spread of communism. He believed that if the United States proved itself not only a powerful but also a compassionate nation, countries of the world would be more likely join the cause of liberty and democracy around the globe.

Kennedy's desire both to help the needy and to fight the spread of communism led to his executive order creating the Peace Corps in March 1961. The

63

Peace Corps program made it possible to strive for these goals and gave Americans an opportunity to live abroad, developing interpersonal and career skills in a foreign culture. The program survives and thrives to this day. Peace Corps volunteers brought education, technology, and an abundance of goodwill to developing nations. Their purpose was to help the people in these countries help themselves. During the Kennedy administration, Peace Corps volunteers brought their knowledge and special training to forty-seven countries. They helped build health centers, schools, bridges, irrigation systems, and power generators, and taught basic reading and writing skills, foreign languages, carpentry, masonry, modern farming techniques, and sanitation methods — just as the volunteers do today. Volunteers lived with a family in the host country, played an active role in the community, and learned a great deal about different ways of life. Today's goals of the Peace Corps are the same as they were when Kennedy created it.

In March 1961, President Kennedy launched a foreign-aid program called The Alliance for Progress, a much more calculating program than Food for Peace or the Peace Corps, but still one that had a humanitarian face. The program was a ten-year plan aimed at keeping the peace in Latin America. The objective was to isolate violent Communist movements already under way there and to stop any others from forming. The Kennedy administration believed that by supplying particular Latin American countries with United States financial support and goods, it could help foil Communist revolutions in those countries.

Kennedy recognized that poor Latin American countries, illiteracy, inadequate housing, unfair land distribution, high inflation, and a lack of schools and sanitation opened doors to communism. Kennedy had long considered political turmoil in Latin America a threat to the security of the United States. He feared that the many revolutionary movements appearing there would establish Communist dictatorships, become friends with the Soviet Union, and threaten liberty in the Western Hemisphere. The Alliance for Progress was an attempt to promote long-term economic growth and social reform in Latin America, thus reducing the likelihood of violent revolution.

President Kennedy was especially concerned about the island nation of Cuba, where, in 1959, a rebel force led by Fidel Castro had overthrown the United States-backed dictator Fulgencio Batista. Under Batista's government, Cuba had been a gold mine for United States businesses, which controlled nearly all of Cuba's utilities, mines, cattle ranches, and oil refineries. Approximately 40 percent of the sugar industry, Cuba's most important business, was controlled by American companies as well. When Castro took over, his government seized more than 1,000,000 acres of land from three American companies and threw them out of the country. As Cuba and the United States became more angry with each other, the Soviet Union sought a friendship with Cuba. Before long, Cuba, only ninety miles

65

off the coast of Florida, became the Soviet Union's partner against the United States.

In early 1960, President Eisenhower directed the Central Intelligence Agency (CIA) to arm and train anti-Castro Cuban citizens living in the United States for a possible invasion of Cuba. Eisenhower feared that if communism took root in Cuba it could spread to the rest of Latin America. These soldiers, or exiles, as they were called, wanted to overthrow Castro's government by force and take back control of Cuba. They also believed that communism was bad for their country. By the time John Kennedy took office, 1,400 fighters were prepared to invade the island. Believing the situation in Cuba to be worsening, he decided to execute the plan. Though in a press conference Kennedy had assured the American people that there would be no invasion of Cuba, plans had already been made to attack. In fact, several reporters, notably from *The New York Times* and *The New Republic*, kept quiet about the story at Kennedy's request.

On April 17, 1961, CIA forces, consisting of the Cuban exiles and a number of Americans, known as the Cuban Brigade, invaded Cuba at the Bay of Pigs, ninety miles from Havana. All United States involvement in the effort was to be kept secret. Kennedy attended a horse-racing event with Jackie and played golf with his brother-in-law during the invasion. The plan was for the CIA-financed forces to hide out in the mountains and encourage a popular uprising against Castro's army, but the Kennedy administration had grossly underestimated Castro's popularity and his army's strength. Within days Castro's army had crushed the CIA forces, capturing or killing all but 150 of the 1,400 invading soldiers, including four American pilots.

Many people blamed President Kennedy for the bungled invasion. He had promised the exiles military help, including air cover to guarantee the success of the invasion, but at the last minute refused to send help. The United States aircraft that did go into battle were broken-down B-26 bombers that anti-Castro Cuban fighters had been flying but were too exhausted to continue. The aircraft, piloted by American volunteers, took part in the invasion, but failed to stop Castro's forces from scoring a clear military victory over the rebel army.

When the extent of United States involvement in the Bay of Pigs invasion became public knowledge, there was widespread protest. Fidel Castro issued an official statement condemning the United States for interfering in Cuba's internal affairs. President Kennedy publicly took full responsibility, but privately he blamed military intelligence for incorrectly estimating the Cuban army's strength.

The Bay of Pigs miscalculation put an abrupt end to the euphoria of Kennedy's first few months in office. Though most Americans stood by their president during the crisis of confidence, many were shocked, not only by the defeat, but also by the fact that Kennedy had lied to them. In Europe, too, there was a great deal of disenchantment with Kennedy. To Europeans, Kennedy had represented the greatest hope for the free world. He now looked to many of them like a clumsy imperialist, trying to impose his political beliefs on others — and failing terribly.

In a single day, and less than four months since his inauguration, the Kennedy image had been tarnished. It was a difficult time for President Kennedy, but the Bay of Pigs taught him to be more cautious. Kennedy tried not to dwell on past failures or successes. He remembered what his father had often said to him and to all the Kennedy children while they were growing up: "That was yesterday. What are you going to do today?"

To shift the public's attention away from the failed Bay of Pigs invasion, Kennedy decided to arrange a meeting with Soviet leader Nikita Khrushchev. Kennedy was generally against summit conferences, or face-to-face meetings with other chiefs of state, unless some specific agreement negotiated at lower levels was awaiting a final approval. However, Kennedy and his advisers believed that an early meeting with the Soviet leader would open channels of communication between the two men, allowing for easier dialogue in the years to come.

The Bay of Pigs fiasco had made April 1961 a very difficult month for Kennedy, and one reason for his wanting to meet with Khrushchev was to forge ahead and try to leave the incident behind him. For the Soviet Union the month of April marked a major Soviet advance in space technology — the first manned orbit of the earth, by Soviet cosmonaut Yuri Gagarin. Khrushchev knew that a superpower summit would be an opportunity to draw world attention to the recent Soviet achievement in space. Since both leaders hoped to bring a little warmth to the Cold War, a summit was arranged for June 3, 1961, in the Western European city of Vienna, Austria.

While flying to Vienna, the Kennedys stopped in Paris, France, to meet with French President Charles De Gaulle. The French, who came out in droves to greet the president and the First Lady, especially loved Jackie, who charmed De Gaulle with her graceful manner and fluent French. There were chants of *"Jah-kie! Jah-kie!"* everywhere she went.

In Vienna, Kennedy and Khrushchev each brought preconceived notions about the other, but they were still eager to seek common ground. In appearance, Kennedy and Khrushchev could not have been more different. Kennedy looked even younger, taller, and more handsome next to the bald, short, and stocky Russian premier. It was their political positions, however, that had to be addressed. Both understood that in addition to the differences in their respective economic systems, there was a competition between the concepts of Western democracy and that of Eastern totalitarianism.

Kennedy and Khrushchev had several brief, but serious discussions, usually at meals, in which they touched on numerous topics. One topic, to no one's surprise, was the Bay of Pigs.

Khrushchev, like most Soviet Communists, based his thinking on the writings of Lenin, the founder of the modern Soviet state. Lenin saw the world as a struggle between communism (the economic system based on common ownership, like that of the Soviet Union) and capitalism (the economic system based on competition and individual ownership, like that of the United States). Khrushchev, like Lenin, believed that communism would eventually win the struggle, and that the entire world would ultimately become one Communist state. Khrushchev even went so far as to proclaim that communism would "bury" capitalism. He said, "There is no longer any force in the world capable of barring the road to [communism]." He further explained to Kennedy that "local wars," like Castro's revolution, were people's liberation movements that could not be stopped because they were steps in history's march toward world communism. Khrushchev also mentioned current conflicts in Southeast Asia and Africa to illustrate his point.

The situation in Southeast Asia to which Khrushchev referred was one that had engaged President Kennedy from his first day in office. In 1954, the United States had joined the Southeast Asia Treaty Organization, a group of nations opposed to, and willing to fight against, the spread of communism in Southeast Asia. In that same year, the Geneva Accords officially ended Vietnam's eight year war of liberation against the French, temporarily dividing the country into North Vietnam and South Vietnam. Vietnam had been a French colony since the 1850s. Ho Chi Minh, a Vietnamese patriot and Communist organizer, established a Communist government in North Vietnam while Ngo Dinh Diem, who opposed communism, became South Vietnam's president. The terms of the treaty included national elections in 1956 to reunify the country.

However, Diem, with the backing of the United States, refused to take part in the national referendum, arguing that North Vietnam would not allow fair elections. President Eisenhower then approved the sending of several hundred American military and civilian advisers to South Vietnam to help strengthen the Diem government. During the next four years, pitched battles were fought between South Vietnamese rebels, or Viet Cong as they were called, and Diem's army. By 1960 Diem had grown increasingly unpopular with the South Vietnamese. At the same time North Vietnamese Communists were threatening to overthrow his government.

As a senator, Kennedy had originally opposed providing military aid to the French while they fought to keep their colonies in Indochina. But after he became president in 1961, Kennedy greatly expanded American economic and military aid to South Vietnam. Like his predecessors, presidents Truman and Eisenhower, Kennedy came to accept the "domino" theory, which predicted that if one country fell to communism, its neighbors would soon meet the same fate.

In the two years and ten months that Kennedy was president he increased the number of military and civilian advisers from about 900 to over 16,000. Although this conflict seemed to be a distant problem — at the time Kennedy was obsessed with Cuba — his decision to expand dramatically America's military involvement in Vietnam lead the United States into the longest war of its history.

71

There was no need for Kennedy to explain to Khrushchev America's intention to fight communism throughout the world. This had been United States policy for many years, and the Soviet leader clearly understood that this policy was not going to change. In fact, Kennedy was very impressed with how thoroughly informed Khrushchev was with regard to Kennedy's own positions, past and present, on specific issues.

When the space program became a topic of conversation, Khrushchev, as expected, boasted about the recent Soviet orbital flight. Kennedy made the Soviet leader a compelling offer. He asked Khrushchev if he would be interested in combining Soviet and United States technologies in a quest for a moon landing. Khrushchev hesitated, then casually responded, "Why not?" The official Soviet position, however, was not one of cooperation, and the two countries would never work together on a mission to reach the moon.

The United States space program, begun shortly after World War II, had always been a low priority with little financial backing. In 1957, when the Soviet Union launched its *Sputnik I* satellite, the sorry state of American space technology and Soviet superiority in that area quickly became apparent. In his inaugural address and his first State of the Union message, Kennedy vowed to put the United States back in the space race. Early in his administration, he put Vice-President Johnson in charge of the National Space Council, increased its funding, and declared in a press conference that it would be in the national interest to put a man on the moon by the end of the decade. On May 5, 1961, just prior to the summit in Vienna, the United States completed a successful manned space flight (a monkey accompanied the astronaut), but the mission did not include orbiting the earth. The Soviets, clearly ahead in the race to the moon, were not eager to cooperate on a moon mission and eventually have to share the glory with the Americans. Such was the Cold War reasoning of the period.

There was more than intense political discussion on the agenda for the two summit delegations. The Austrian government had arranged a state dinner for its guests. Though the dinner was a formal affair, the Soviet delegation, as always, wore business suits. To the Soviets, trappings of wealth that Americans consider fairly commonplace — tuxedos, furs, jewelry — make a mockery of the struggles of working-class people. Though by American standards seriously underdressed for the occasion, the stout Khrushchev, who was of Ukrainian peasant stock, was quite comfortable in his baggy, roughly tailored suit.

There were a few light moments at the affair. Soviet Premier Khrushchev especially enjoyed speaking with Jackie Kennedy. They chatted on various topics, including the space program and a particular Soviet flight in which dogs were sent into the outer atmosphere. Noting that the dogs had since given birth to a litter of puppies, Jackie asked Khrushchev how the newborns were doing. Two months later, a frightened little dog was delivered by a Soviet messenger to the White House — a gift from Premier Khrushchev. Puzzled, Kennedy asked his wife why the Soviet leader had sent the puppy. After Jackie explained, the president decided it was smart foreign policy to accept the gift graciously.

A very important and extremely sensitive issue discussed at the summit concerned the German city of Berlin, the original German capital. Since the Allied defeat of the Germans in World War II, Germany had been split into Western and Soviet sectors, East and West Germany. The western part of Berlin had been controlled by the West, even though it was located within Soviet-controlled East Germany.

The difference between the depressed eastern part of the city and the thriving western part had created a problem for the Soviets. Many East Germans, a significant number of them skilled professionals and technicians, had already crossed the border in search of greater political freedom and economic opportunity. In July 1961 alone, more than 30,000 East Germans had fled to the West. The Soviets wanted the entire city to be Communist and had made numerous unsuccessful efforts to stop the exodus of its people.

At the summit, Khrushchev and Kennedy could not agree on the Berlin issue, and the Soviet leader made vague threats. As the two leaders bade their last good-byes, Kennedy said to Khrushchev, "It will be a cold winter."

Late that summer, on Soviet orders, East German troops built a stone wall fortified with barbed wire along the border in an effort to stop East Germans from leaving East Berlin. Government officials in West Berlin requested the aid of United States soldiers, so President Kennedy sent 1,500 United States troops to patrol the primary route entering Berlin from West Germany. By the end of August, Soviet and United States troops and tanks were poised on each side of the Berlin Wall. Within twenty-four hours Soviet forces withdrew, but the Cold War continued, and the Berlin Wall would remain a symbol of Soviet repression to this day.

Many historians agree that in the first year of the Kennedy administration, America faced more crisis situations than in the first year of any previous administration. Despite the difficult year, the mood at the White House was very upbeat. The presence of the Kennedy children, John and Caroline, was clearly responsible for a lot of the optimism. While the superpowers wrestled behind the scenes, Americans continued to fall under the spell of the Kennedy family.

President Kennedy had faced some very tough situations that year. He had been able to restore the credibility he had squandered in the Bay of Pigs invasion by taking full responsibility for the failure. He had regained the confidence of the American public by representing his country well at the Vienna summit and by standing tough against fellow Cold Warrior Khrushchev. Also, in Berlin, he had shown the world that the United States intended to honor its commitments to the free world. However, that year fate once more handed John Kennedy a personal tragedy — his father, Joseph, Sr., suffered a severe stroke just before Christmas while playing golf in Palm Beach. The stroke paralyzed Joseph's right side and badly impaired his speech. The elder Kennedy's failing health might have been an omen of more difficulties ahead for the Kennedy administration, for in 1962 the president was asked to apply in Asia the lessons he had learned from the Bay of Pigs disaster.

In 1949, Chinese leader Mao Zedong had brought communism to China in one of the few peasant revolutions of the twentieth century. In the process, the former leader Chiang Kai-shek retreated to the island of Formosa, or Taiwan, where he established a government in exile. Until his death in 1975, Chiang claimed that his nationalist government was the truly legitimate government of China. Because of Mao's interest in spreading communism throughout Asia, the United States supported Chiang's claim. In 1962, China was experiencing economic difficulties at home and strained relations with the Soviet Union, and Chiang saw it as a good time to invade the mainland.

To Kennedy, the China-Formosa conflict was very similar to the situation that had prevailed in Cuba during the spring of 1961. There, too, was a small group of exiled nationalists, forced to leave their country by a Communist revolution and eager to reclaim power by force. This time, however, Kennedy recognized that the exiled forces were too small to succeed without the help of massive American forces. Not wanting to make the mistake he had made in Cuba, Kennedy informed Chiang Kai-shek that the

United States would not participate in an invasion of mainland China.

Chiang knew he could not succeed without considerable United States support, but he would not take no for an answer. In order to embarrass Kennedy into joining the planned invasion, Chiang began publicizing his intentions and what he characterized as a United States willingness to let communism thrive and spread through Asia. Rather than wait to be invaded, the Chinese Communists, stating clearly that Formosa was always part of China, prepared to attack the rebels and rid themselves of Chiang once and for all. Though he had declined to assist Chiang in an offensive action, President Kennedy would not sit by and allow the Chinese to advance communism beyond its borders. Kennedy immediately made clear his intention to defend Formosa against any attack, and the Chinese retreated.

In October 1962, Kennedy faced another challenge. China troops crossed into India, a severe escalation of a continuing border conflict, and Kennedy was called on once more to show that the United States was willing to mount a defense against Communist expansion. At the request of Indian Prime Minister Jawaharlal Nehru, Kennedy ordered the delivery of weapons to India, and the United States joined Great Britain in an agreement to provide India with an air defense. The Chinese, again, retreated.

While Kennedy was struggling with communism on the other side of the globe, he was also dealing with a Communist threat in America's backyard. On October 15, 1962, President Kennedy was informed that there were Soviet missile bases, and perhaps nuclear warheads, in Cuba. The failure of the Bay of Pigs invasion ha dcome back to haunt him in the form of the Cuban missile crisis. For the first time in history the world stood on the brink of nuclear war, but Kennedy, through his unique combination of courage and restraint, preserved the peace.

Reflecting on the missile crisis, his brother Robert Kennedy later wrote:

> The fourteen people involved [in the Executive Committee] were very . . . bright, able, dedicated people, all of whom had the greatest affection for the United States. . . . If six of them had been president of the United States, I think that the world might have been blown up.

As it turned out, the world was not blown up, and Kennedy was eager to bring the countries of the world closer together. He decided to go to Berlin, the point at which East and West stood face to face with only the ugly, threatening Berlin Wall between them.

Always prepared, Kennedy read several books on Germany and its history before making the trip. He had mixed expectations. Would the German people be more likely to remember how American forces devastated their cities in World War II? Or would they be grateful for the goodwill the United States extended by helping to rebuild their economy after the war? Had the resentment been passed on through generations? Or were the German people looking toward a brighter future despite the past? He would soon know the answers to these questions.

A 1963 Gallup Poll rated the president's popularity in America at 76 percent. That year, on June 23, Kennedy left for Germany, hoping to strengthen his image abroad and to translate that popularity into pro-American sentiment.

President Kennedy was very well received in Frankfurt, the industrial heartland of Germany. He spoke about "a united Europe in an Atlantic partnership," and promised that "the United States will risk its cities to defend yours because we need your freedom to protect ours."

On June 26, Kennedy spoke before 150,000 West Berliners, more than half the city's entire population. The reception they gave him was overwhelming, even extraordinary. Berliners of all ages filled the streets, waving, singing, clapping, and calling out his name. They were a threatened people. Their city was torn in half by a hostile political act — the building of the Berlin Wall — and they knew Kennedy was there because he understood their plight.

Upon his arrival, Kennedy had visited the Berlin Wall and had been deeply affected by its grotesque, imposing presence. Looking out over the crowded streets from the speaker's platform, Kennedy could see in the people's faces both faith and fear. He knew that for them he represented hope for a future free from the threat of communism. The people's voices were so emotional, the mood so powerful, that several Kennedy aides were moved to tears as they stood on the platform. Then Kennedy began to speak:

There are many people in the world who really
don't understand, or say they don't, what is the
great issue between the free world and the Communist world. Let them come to Berlin! There are
some who say that communism is the wave of the
future. Let them come to Berlin! . . . And there are
even a few who say that it is true that communism
is an evil system, but it permits us to make economic progress. . . .

Freedom has many difficulties and democracy is
not perfect, but we have never had to put a wall up to
keep our people in. . . . All free men, wherever they
may live, are citizens of Berlin, and therefore, as a
free man, I take pride in the words, "Ich bin ein
Berliner."

President Kennedy did not speak German well,
but when he proclaimed "I am a Berliner" in their
language he charmed the citizens of West Berlin for
all time. Once again his deft delivery of a brilliant
phrase captured the hearts and minds of millions of
people.

When Kennedy and his aides boarded Air Force
One for the flight home, the president was proud that
he had done what was necessary to keep West Berlin
free. The West Berliners had opened their hearts to
him, and he would never forget either the pain or the
joy in their faces. As he leaned back in his seat,
Kennedy said to an aide, "We'll never have another
day like this one as long as we live."

After the overwhelming response Kennedy received in West Berlin, he returned home to face a

long-simmering domestic problem — civil rights. In a speech to the nation just before his trip to Germany, Kennedy said,

> We preach freedom around the world, and we mean it, and we cherish our freedom here at home — but are we to say to the world and, much more importantly, to each other that this is a land of the free except for Negroes; that we have no second-class citizens except Negroes; that we have no class or caste system, no ghettos, no master race except with respect to Negroes?

One of President Kennedy's greatest challenges — proving that America is indeed a place where everyone has equal opportunity under the law — now lay before him.

7

Kennedy's Fight for Civil Rights

IN FEBRUARY 1960, four black college freshmen in Greensboro, North Carolina, sat down at a "whites only" lunch counter at a Woolworth's store and asked if they could order something to eat. They were not surprised when the owner of the store refused to serve them simply because they were black. Though they were insulted and ridiculed by the white people there, the students remained at the counter, refusing to leave until they were served lunch. Unwilling to give in to the students' demands, the owner closed the counter for the rest of the afternoon. When they returned the next day, the students again received the same ill treatment. Undaunted, they returned the next day and again each day after that until they were finally served.

During the early 1960s, the Kennedy administration had to deal with a number of domestic crises, the most important being racial violence. The civil rights movement and the country's resistance to it became the domestic focus of Kennedy's first months in office. In 1960, about 55 percent of the black families in the United States were living below the poverty level. The civil rights movement was an all-out effort of black and white Americans to overcome the racial injustice that had increased that poverty. White families, too, were poor, but for blacks the problem was more widespread and had definite, identifiable causes.

The heart of the problem was racism. Racism, or the hatred one might feel toward another person simply because that person has a different racial background from one's own, is usually caused by a fear of people unlike ourselves. Anyone, regardless of color, can feel racial hatred. Today, because of the influence of the civil rights movement, most of us know that it is everyone's job to overcome such feelings, both in one's self and in others. In the 1960s, however, America was a country still trying to rise above its own racist fears.

Civil rights became an important issue across America in the early 1960s. The issue was most critical in the South, where segregation, or separation, of blacks and whites in public places dominated every aspect of social and business life. Black students attended their own schools, which were inferior to those attended by whites. Education was so lacking for black Americans that it was almost impossible for them to learn the necessary skills to become doctors, teachers, or other professionals. Instead blacks were forced to earn their living by working at low-paying, unskilled jobs. Without a good education, the daily lives of black Americans and their children had little prospect for change.

Housing and medical care were also substandard in black communities. Black Americans in rural communities usually lived in run-down shacks, often without floors. In American cities, blacks crowded into poorly heated apartment buildings where hoards of rats and mice made the already unsanitary conditions even worse. When these living conditions brought on sickness, there was little or no medical attention to be had. Because of the high cost of such care, most black Americans were unable to afford health insurance. They often suffered their illnesses without the attention of a doctor. While there were whites who lived at this level of poverty, they were never denied housing or medical attention because of their race, as were the blacks.

Though segregation existed throughout the United States, in much of the South it seeped into many aspects of society. Blacks were only allowed to use "colored" seats on buses and trains, always at the back. Only certain restaurants would serve black customers, and even then, only at designated tables or counter seats. Blacks were forced to take the freight elevators in some department stores and office buildings, and had separate entrances at movie theaters. Only the most unpleasant jobs were available to blacks, usually at a lower wage than a white person in the same position. In general, it was a common practice to deny a person a seat, a meal, an education, a job, and even a drink of water just because he or she was black.

The Supreme Court, in a landmark decision, had ordered the desegregation of public schools in 1954, prohibiting discrimination on the basis of race. But changing the law was easier than changing some people's way of thinking. Many people resisted desegregation, refusing to obey the law, and often this resistance led to violence.

President Kennedy, a son of a millionaire, had always lived a life of privilege, but the homeless, the hungry, and the uneducated were not strangers to him when he took office. He had witnessed poverty first-hand during his campaign travels, when he had visited black families living in cramped, run-down housing, with little money for food or clothing. On the campaign trail, he had expressed his concern for the plight of black Americans in one of his speeches: "The Negro baby born in America today," he said, "has about one-half as much chance of completing high school as a white baby born in the same place on the same day, one-third as much chance of completing college . . . a life expectancy which is seven years shorter, and the prospects of earning only half as much."

Perhaps what made the Kennedy administration's struggle against racism most difficult was that racial prejudice is learned and passed down within the family. Many people, particularly in the South, believed that the separation of the races was a perfectly acceptable social arrangement. Not only did they see nothing wrong with segregation, but they believed that integration, or the mixing of the races, was unnatural and, some even believed, sinful or evil. Fortunately, many whites believed that segregation was immoral and needed to be abolished.

Though Kennedy supported desegregation, as he said he would during his presidential campaign, Congress was much less in favor of the idea. Senators and representatives from the South, in particular, did not want to offend the people in their states who had voted for them by passing laws that would make segregation illegal. Kennedy knew that any such legislation he might propose in the form of a civil rights bill would probably be rejected by Congress. He feared that by confronting Congress on unpopular issues so early in his term, he would ruin his chances of getting other important legislation passed. Not one to be thwarted, Kennedy decided to try another tactic.

The president was concerned about the extent to which blacks had been denied equal opportunities in the different branches of the government and the military. He instructed his Cabinet members to report on the racial balance of their departments. When he discovered that few blacks held important jobs, Kennedy set out to correct the situation and advance the cause of civil rights by appointing blacks to various positions in his administration. During his time as president there was a marked increase in the number of blacks serving in high government positions.

The results of Kennedy's efforts were especially evident in the Department of Justice and in the court system. When Kennedy took office, there were no black attorneys in the Department of Justice. By the end of his presidency there were seventy. Kennedy appointed black United States attorneys, black federal judges, and the first black female judge, Marjorie Lawson. His appointment of Judge Thurgood Marshall to the Court of Appeals led to President Johnson's 1967 appointment of Marshall as the ninety-sixth, and first black, Justice of the United States Supreme Court, the highest level of the federal judiciary system.

For millions of black Americans, the efforts of the Kennedy administration, though considerable, were not advancing the cause of racial equality fast enough. In the 1950s, many black Americans had begun to practice civil disobedience in order to draw attention to the injustices they suffered and to force change. During the 1960s, an increasing number of Americans, both black and white, began to practice civil disobedience. "Sit-in" demonstrations like the one in Greensboro became more frequent and involved more participants in cities large and small throughout the South until the civil rights movement was born. In 1960 alone more than 50,000 people, mostly black, participated in demonstrations, and more than 3,600 people were jailed for civil rights activities.

Civil disobedience took many forms. Throughout the South and elsewhere, blacks rode in "whites only" sections of buses, used "whites only" rest rooms, and demanded service in "whites only" restaurants, all in an effort to draw attention to the injustice of racial discrimination. The demonstrations, though they started out peacefully, often ended in violent clashes with white racists, and the civil rights movement became an even more difficult struggle.

More than any other individual, Dr. Martin Luther King, Jr., gave the civil rights movement the leadership it needed to move forward. Dr. King, a Baptist minister, had grown up in the Deep South and had known virtually every form of racial discrimination and humiliation. During the early 1950s, he had led numerous mass demonstrations in Georgia and Alabama. He had been stabbed, beaten, arrested, and jailed for his activities, and in 1957 *Time* magazine did a cover story on him. By the time John Kennedy was elected president, Dr. King was the nationally recognized leader of the civil rights movement.

Dr. King believed that much could be accomplished by civil disobedience, or active, yet nonviolent resistance. He had been greatly influenced by the teachings of Indian political and spiritual leader Mohandas K. Gandhi. By organizing mass demonstrations of civil disobedience, Gandhi had helped India achieve its independence from Great Britain in 1947. Dr. King hoped to win equality for black Americans through the use of sit-ins and boycotts. Dr. King condemned violence and preached many times that violence only bred more violence.

One such demonstration began on May 4, 1961, when white and black "freedom riders" boarded buses in Washington, D.C., and set off on a long journey through the South. Using "whites only" public rest rooms and lunch counters along the way, the freedom riders hoped to reach the port city of New Orleans, Louisiana, but they never got there. Though their goal was to demonstrate peacefully at every stop, the freedom riders found themselves on a collision course with southern racists.

First, a bus was smashed and fire-bombed by local residents in Anniston, Alabama. Then their attackers held the doors of the bus closed as the freedom riders struggled to get out of the burning bus. When the demonstrators finally forced their way out, just before the bus exploded, the crazed racists beat the passengers with pipes, bicycle chains, and baseball bats. Then, unbelievably, many of the burned and beaten demonstrators were denied treatment at a local hospital.

In Birmingham, Alabama, another group of freedom riders was attacked in a similar fashion. On neither occasion did the local police or the FBI, which was also present, act to defend the demonstrators.

In Montgomery, Alabama, another group of freedom riders that had come from Nashville, Tennessee, met with similar violence. Realizing that local officials were either unable or unwilling to stop the violence, the Kennedy administration took action. Attorney General Robert Kennedy contacted Alabama politicians, including the governor, and urged them to order local police to protect civil rights demonstrators from racist attackers. He was surprised, however, when they resisted his order. President Kennedy sent a special representative to Montgomery, but even he was attacked by a racist mob and beaten unconscious. Again, the FBI merely observed. President Kennedy, however, was reluctant to put more pressure on southern politicians to act. Robert Kennedy helped to convince the president to put aside politics and take action. Robert said that injustice and racial hatred were dividing the country and that the beatings of peaceful demonstrators had to be stopped. Finally, the president and the attorney general, despite the governor's strong resistance, sent 600 federal marshals to Alabama, and order was restored. The passengers, who had been jailed for their own safety, were released.

A year later, thanks to the freedom riders, desegregation of interstate travel became a reality. An Interstate Commerce Commission regulation banned segregation on buses, trains, and airlines so that blacks could travel with as much freedom as whites. The regulation, however, represented only a small victory for civil rights activists; the struggle for racial equality was far from over.

The denial of voting rights was one of the many ways racists controlled and suppressed black Americans. Though it was an obvious violation of a black person's constitutional rights to prevent a registered black voter admission to a voting booth on Election Day, this was often done. Southern racists also used other illegal methods to undermine the Constitution. For example, blacks were required to pay poll taxes and to pass reading tests before they could register, while taxes and tests were not required of whites. Because blacks for years had been denied decent jobs and education, they were often too poor to be able to afford the tax or were too uneducated to pass the reading test. In this way, blacks were denied their right to vote and, thus, their power to change the system by working within the system. Frequently, blacks who tried to register to vote met with racist violence. Some who persisted were killed.

President Kennedy, who had received 75 percent of the black vote in the very close 1960 presidential election, considered the voting rights of black Americans an extremely important issue. His administration supported the efforts of local groups and foundations in voter-registration drives throughout the South.

Also, under the direction of Attorney General Robert Kennedy, the Justice Department made the voting rights of black Americans a top priority and filed numerous lawsuits involving violations of those rights. President Kennedy reasoned that the power of the black vote could eventually end segregation, since black voters would elect senators and representatives who supported the civil rights movement. He also knew that a larger pool of black voters was likely to help him in his campaign for reelection in 1964.

Still, many people criticized President Kennedy for not moving quickly enough on the issue of civil rights. They urged him to propose legislation that would make racial discrimination illegal and that would integrate schools. He continued to hesitate, believing that any such proposal would cause friction in the government at a time when the country could not afford bad relations between his administration and the country's lawmakers. Finally, in the fall of 1962, the forty-five-year-old president found he had no choice but to move forward aggressively on the civil rights issue, even though many key senators and representatives were publicly criticizing the civil rights movement as mob violence.

In September 1962, a black Air Force veteran named James Meredith attempted to become the first black student to enroll at the University of Mississippi. The university had admitted him but then had refused to permit him to attend classes when it discovered he was black. When Meredith took his case to court, the judge ordered that he be allowed to go to school, but when he showed up to register for his courses he faced racist protesters, including the governor himself, who blocked the school's entrance.

Attorney General Robert Kennedy failed to convince the Mississippi governor of Meredith's right to attend the all-white university, so the attorney general decided to ask federal marshals to escort Meredith past the demonstrators and into the school's registration building. To make the process as peaceful as possible, Robert Kennedy had his assistants arrange for the registration to take place on September 30, a Sunday night, when the campus was normally quiet.

That afternoon crowds gathered in front of the university's administration building to protest Meredith's registration. As evening approached, the crowd grew larger and became angry and restless.

When the attorney general's assistants and the marshals arrived, it looked as if their efforts to register Meredith peacefully were going to end in violence. They were right.

Several protesters threw stones and bottles at the marshals. Then gunshots were fired. The marshals responded by throwing canisters of tear gas, but the protesters only intensified their efforts to block the registration as the tear gas wore off. Having decided not to tolerate further racial violence in the South, President Kennedy sent in the National Guard. When the incident was finally over, two people had been killed, and twenty-nine marshals and thirteen members of the Mississippi National Guard had been shot. Meredith registered for classes the following morning.

President Kennedy went on television to announce proudly the registration of the first black student at the University of Mississippi. He said that Meredith's registration represented a triumph of fairness over racial hatred, a victory for the law of the land over mob violence. But the violence at the University of Mississippi had shocked President Kennedy and his brother. They wondered how people could hate so intensely. The Meredith affair opened the Kennedy brothers' eyes to the deep racial hatred that existed in the United States. They decided to do whatever was possible to bring about racial harmony in America. In the spring of 1963, President Kennedy was forced to deal with still more racial violence in the South. In April a nonviolent demonstration in Birmingham, Alabama, led by Dr. Martin

Luther King, Jr., turned into a clash between demonstrators and the police. Led by Sheriff Eugene "Bull" Connor, who was also a Birmingham mayoral candidate, the police beat the protesters with clubs and fire hoses and arrested hundreds of them. Dr. King was among those arrested. He announced that the demonstrations would continue until lunch counters and rest rooms were integrated, until blacks were hired by certain local businesses, and until a committee made up of blacks and whites was established to plan the desegregation of Birmingham. Sheriff Connor responded bitterly by saying that "blood would run in the streets" before integration would come to his city.

The violence in Birmingham continued. On Good Friday, Dr. King, who had been released from jail, led fifty demonstrators through the city. They were arrested within minutes, and he was placed in jail in solitary confinement. While Dr. King was imprisoned, he read a letter published in a Birmingham newspaper. Signed by eight white Christian and Jewish members of the clergy, the letter was a plea to the black community to stop demonstrating and take its case to court. Dr. King personally responded to the editorial. His "Letter from a Birmingham Jail" was smuggled out of the prison by Dr. King's lawyers and published by concerned citizens. It was immediately acknowledged as the most eloquent expression of the philosophy and goals of the civil rights movement.

Also, while Dr. King was in jail, his younger brother recruited demonstrators at nightly church meetings and eventually led 1,500 of them through the Birmingham streets. Thanks to the efforts of singer Harry Belafonte, who managed to raise $50,000 in contributions, Dr. King and the demonstrators were bailed out of jail.

For President Kennedy and many other Americans, the movement became even more powerful on May 1, 1963, when 1,000 children marched into downtown Birmingham, singing songs for freedom. City police arrested hundreds of them. The next day more than 2,000 children marched, carrying signs and chanting. Sheriff Connor dispatched the fire department to the scene and had them turn high-pressure water hoses on the young people. Snarling police dogs were then used to force the demonstrators to retreat.

In a spirit of unity with the imprisoned protesters, more than 3,000 people demonstrated at Birmingham jail on May 5 in a mass prayer meeting. They kneeled down along Sheriff Connor's police barricades. When the sheriff ordered the fire hoses to be turned on the demonstrators, the firefighters, fed up with Connor's brutal tactics, parted and allowed the protesters to demonstrate freely. Reporters on the scene wrote that there were tears in the eyes of some of the firefighters. Americans were shocked when television news broadcasts brought the Birmingham violence into their living rooms. When they saw Sheriff Bull Connor's vicious police dogs biting black women, and schoolchildren being thrown into buildings and through store windows by the force of the water from the fire hoses, Americans were outraged and demanded an end to racial violence. The public outcry that President Kennedy had been hoping for had finally occurred. The president later remarked on the irony of the situation: "The civil rights movement should thank God for Bull Connor. He's helped it as much as Abraham Lincoln," whose Emancipation Proclamation had freed the slaves in 1863.

President Kennedy sent in 3,000 troops in an all-out effort to restore order in Birmingham. The violence stopped for the time being. However, the Kennedy administration had made a new enemy — Alabama Governor George Wallace.

In the summer of 1963, Wallace, whose motto was "Segregation Now! Segregation Tomorrow! Segregation Forever!," vowed to block the registration of black students at Alabama State University. Attorney General Robert Kennedy persuaded several of the state's business leaders to discourage the governor from doing so. The president, who was firmly committed to school integration, threatened to use troops to overcome Governor Wallace's resistance. On June 11, 1963, the governor appeared at the university's entrance, but he was only bluffing. He stepped aside to allow the students, escorted by a Justice Department official, to enter the campus.

To no one's surprise, President Kennedy's popularity in the South plummeted. Southern whites blamed the Kennedy administration for causing the racial conflicts in their states, while some blacks complained that the president was not acting swiftly enough to end segregation. Attorney General Robert Kennedy, the focus of much of the criticism, offered to resign his post, but the president asked him to stay on. The president knew that his brother Robert was as committed as he was to furthering the civil rights movement.

The nation was divided along racial lines, and John Kennedy was determined to bring the country back together. He believed the best way to begin was to address the American people directly. President Kennedy once again went on television. He reminded the nation of the promise of President Lincoln's Emancipation Proclamation. "Now the time has come for this nation to fulfill its promise," Kennedy said. "We face a moral crisis as a country and as a people. . . . It cannot be met by repressive police action. It cannot be left to increased demonstrations in the streets. It cannot be quieted by token moves or talk. It is time to act. . . . A great change is at hand, and our task, our obligation, is to make that revolution, that change, peaceful and constructive for all." Finally, President Kennedy told the television audience that he was sending a comprehensive civil rights bill to Congress.

The violence in Alabama continued. In September 1963, four young black girls were killed when a Baptist church in Birmingham was bombed by the Ku Klux Klan, a white racist group known for its many acts of racial violence, primarily in the South. A joint funeral was held for three of the girls, and Reverend Martin Luther King, Jr., gave the eulogy, calling them "heroines of a holy crusade for freedom and human dignity."

With the exception of Robert Kennedy, the president's cabinet advisers did not think the time was right to ask Congress to pass a civil rights bill. They believed that southern members of Congress, despite the growing public outcry against racial violence, were still inclined to block any civil rights legislation. President Kennedy believed, however, that there had been so much violence, and that public sentiment was so strongly in his favor, that Congress would have to support him on the civil rights bill on popular demand, if not out of good conscience.

The bill's chances of passing did not seem to be good. A few hours after President Kennedy's speech, a prominent civil rights leader, Medgar Evers, was shot to death in front of his home in Jackson, Mississippi. The next day a number of Southern senators announced that they would work to block the president's civil rights bill.

Despite such threats to defeat integration, the president presented a detailed civil rights bill to Congress on June 19, 1963. The bill contained two basic provisions. One was a ban on racial discrimination in public places, including restaurants, hotels, retail stores, and other places connected with interstate commerce. The other provision gave the attorney general the authority to take whatever actions he felt necessary to desegregate public schools.

President Kennedy knew that passage of the bill would require votes from both Republican and Democratic senators. He began an all-out effort to push the bill through. First he asked the Congress, "Look into your hearts . . . for the one plain, proud, and priceless quality that unites all Americans: a sense of justice." Then he contacted many of the nation's most influential leaders in labor and business and asked them for their support. Clergy members from all faiths announced they were in favor of Congress's passing the bill, agreeing with the president that racial violence had to be stopped by whatever means possible.

Robert Kennedy spent many hours each day on the phone with southern politicians and lawyers, trying to convince them that racial equality was best for the country. He pointed out the absurd fact that some restaurants and hotels in Georgia allowed dogs but not black people on their premises. As President Kennedy hoped and expected, the American public, too, called for Congress to pass the bill.

To the president's delight, many people responded to his proposal of the civil rights bill by taking their own civil rights initiative. Voluntary desegregation began to occur throughout the South. Restaurant owners integrated their rest rooms and began to serve blacks and whites alike. The "whites only" signs were taken down at theaters and other public establishments, and even some school districts began programs for desegregating their schools.

Progress was slow, but the president was encouraged. He realized that even if it passed, the civil rights bill alone would not put an end to racial injustice. The civil rights movement was a social revolution. An enormous change had to take place in people's hearts and minds before it could take place in their homes and neighborhoods. Such a revolution had to occur slowly, but simply that it was in fact taking place was reason to be encouraged.

While the civil rights bill was being debated in Congress, civil rights protesters continued to demonstrate across the country. Sit-ins were extremely common at lunch counters and on public transportation. The movement continued rapidly to gain strength.

On August 28, 1963, a combination of civil rights groups, churches, and unions planned to hold a peaceful demonstration at the Lincoln Memorial in Washington, D.C. It would be called the March on Washington and was expected to be the biggest civil rights demonstration yet. Reverend Martin Luther King, Jr., discussed the idea of the demonstration with President Kennedy.

Kennedy was against the March on Washington, fearing that it might cause some senators to vote against the civil rights bill. The president also feared that very few people would absent themselves from jobs and families and travel great distances to Washington, D.C., for such an event, and that as a result of a small turnout the demonstration would be a flop and possibly be ridiculed in the press. Finally, and most troublesome for the president, was the possibility that the demonstration might become violent. He had seen the bloodshed that could result from a relatively small demonstration. The potential for tragedy at such a large demonstration was great indeed. The American Nazi party had already threatened to hold a demonstration of its own, protesting the civil rights movement.

Kennedy told Dr. King that the march was "ill-timed." When Dr. King told him that the March was proceeding as planned, the president, though he declined an offer to speak at the demonstration, ordered the attorney general's office to supply food, outdoor toilets, and paper cups for the marchers. He wanted to be more supportive, but he feared the reaction his approval might create in Congress and throughout the South.

As it turned out, the president had to supply many more cups than he had anticipated. More than 200,000 pro-civil rights activists, both black and white, arrived in Washington for the event. There was music, poetry, prayers, and speeches — and no violence. The March on Washington was not only by far the largest demonstration in the movement's history, but it was the largest public demonstration ever held in Washington, D.C. That day Dr. King delivered his "I Had a Dream" speech, a persuasive and passionate plea for racial justice. Relying on the public speaking skills he had developed as a Baptist minister, he brought the civil rights movement to an emotional peak. Dr. King, would win the Nobel Prize for Peace the following year for preaching nonviolence as a means of achieving equality.

Soon after the March on Washington, President Kennedy met with Dr. King and several other civil rights leaders at the White House. The president was proud of the way the demonstrators had conducted themselves and was impressed with their convic-

President Kennedy was known as an ardent supporter of the civil rights movement. He is shown here meeting with the leaders of the March on Washington, a day-long demonstration held on August 28, 1963. Among them is Reverend Martin Luther King, Jr. (far left), who delivered his famed "I have a dream..." speech to the more than 200,000 people who gathered.

tion. He praised the demonstrators for their "deep fervor and quiet dignity."

Kennedy doubted that the March had opened the minds of many southern racists, and did not think any southern senators would vote differently on the civil rights bill as a result of what they had seen at the Lincoln Memorial that day. Even so, President Kennedy believed that the demonstration had been a success. Because the March on Washington had been an enormous, yet peaceful demonstration, the demonstrators had earned a degree of respect for the civil rights movement. After a long and heated debate in Congress, numerous demonstrations, and countless incidents of racial violence across the country, the president's civil rights bill was eventually passed by the legislature on July 2, 1964.

Several weeks after the March on Washington, President Kennedy read a book called *The Other America: Poverty in the United States*, by Michael Harrington. It concluded that about one-fifth of the nation lived at a substandard level. The book so moved the president that the problem of poverty in America quickly became one of the chief domestic concerns of his administration.

While many Americans in the early 1960s were living comfortably, the president would not ignore the poorer element of American society. In early November,he remarked to White House aide Arthur Schlesinger, Jr., "The time has come to organize a national assault on the causes of poverty, a comprehensive program, across the board."

The president wanted to introduce legislation that would create jobs and businesses for people whose incomes were low. He realized that social programs such as these would be costly and might seem threatening to the middle class, which, with its hard-earned tax dollars, paid the bulk of federal costs. His plan, therefore, had to provide something not only for the poor, but for the middle class as well.

President Kennedy instructed his Treasury Secretary Douglas Dillon and economic adviser Walter Heller to create a such a program. There were already a number of government programs to help the poor, but they were scattered and disorganized. To wage a real war on poverty, Kennedy's aides believed, the federal government had to stimulate community action at the lowest levels. The poorest Americans in the very poorest neighborhoods had to be shown how to help themselves break the poverty cycle. The first step was to instill hope where there had been only despair. For the middle class, there had to be tax reductions.

President Kennedy knew that poverty would not be eliminated quickly, but he was determined to set the wheels in motion. The president told his brother Robert that during his second term he would concentrate on domestic affairs, and especially the problems of the poor. The dream of America's impoverished had become his dream as well.

But President John Kennedy would not live to see his visions of freedom and opportunity for all become a reality. For the Kennedy era would end prematurely, during the course of a few seconds, in Dallas, Texas.

8

Death in Dallas

THE DECEMBER 1963 issue of *Redbook* magazine contained an article in which European children were invited to talk about America. To the question "What are Americans like?" one child responded, "The average American is, of course, a Texan. He eats lots of breakfast and gets fat so he has to go on a diet because he likes to look skinny. He calls everyone 'sweetheart' and is bad to colored people. If he doesn't like who is his president, he usually shoots him."

Dallas, Texas, was not a friendly place in 1963 for a liberal politician like John Kennedy. The city had become a thriving oil capital virtually overnight, and its newfound wealth created a boom in the banking, real estate, and insurance industries. The city's population in 1963, which had nearly tripled since 1940, consisted almost entirely of white-collar professionals, and many of its citizens were religious fundamentalists. Dallas was a city bordering on the right-wing fringe, characterized by rigid attitudes and values. The majority of the people of Dallas were absolutely convinced that the Kennedy administration was ruining the country.

The state of Texas had the highest homicide rate in the United States in 1963, twice the national average. By November of that year, when President Kennedy was to visit Dallas, there had already been ninety-eight murders there.

Adlai Stevenson had visited Dallas in October 1963 to attend a United Nations Day ceremony. An organization of ultra-rightists held their own "United States Day" to condemn the Kennedy administration for what they considered its various "treasonous acts." Suddenly, the crowd became violent. Stevenson was hit with a sign bearing an anti-Kennedy slogan. He was spat on, screamed at, and ridiculed before being rescued from the mob by the Dallas police. He asked the police officers, "Are these human beings or are these animals?" Stevenson told the president that "there was something very ugly and frightening about the atmosphere" in Dallas. Several advisers suggested that Kennedy cancel his planned visit to the city.

The president was fully aware that his policies were not especially popular in other parts of Texas as well. Many Texas conservatives believed Kennedy was soft on communism and too interested in helping black Americans. Texans had even disowned Vice-President Johnson, their native son. Still, the president was confident that he could change the people's minds. Kennedy believed that he could convince the people of Texas that he had consistently run his administration with the entire country's best interests in mind. He scheduled a tour of several cities in eastern Texas.

President and Mrs. Kennedy first flew to the city of San Antonio, Texas, where they were very well received. In his public address, Kennedy once more defined the New Frontier. He said, "It refers to this nation's place in history, the fact that we do stand on the edge of a great new era, filled with both crisis and opportunity, an era to be characterized by achievement and by challenge. It is an era that calls for action and for the best efforts of all those who would test the unknown and the uncertain in every phase of human endeavor."

Despite President Kennedy's sagging popularity in Texas, Jackie, always a hit wherever she and her husband went, enjoyed celebrity status in the Lone Star State. Knowing this, in his speech in San Antonio the president quipped, "Two years ago I introduced myself in Paris by saying I was the man who accompanied Mrs. Kennedy to Paris. I am getting somewhat the same sensation as I travel around Texas. Why is it nobody wonders what Lyndon and I will be wearing?" The president was referring to the fact that Mrs. Kennedy had become a popular trendsetter since coming to the White House. Young women everywhere had taken to imitating the First Lady, wearing their hair like Jackie's and pill-box hats like the one she wore. America loved its First

Lady, and the people of San Antonio seemed no exception that day.

When the Kennedys went on to Houston, Jackie spoke Spanish to a crowd that included many Spanish-speaking Americans. The people were overjoyed to hear her fluent Spanish, and she was extremely happy to be so well received. To the president's delight, Jackie began to like politics more and more, and even mentioned to a Kennedy aide that she was looking forward to campaigning for her husband's reelection in 1964.

Fort Worth proved to be just as receptive to the presidential party as the previous cities on the tour. Hundreds of people turned out to hear Kennedy speak. Because Jackie loved painting, an art exhibit in her honor was set up in the hotel lobby where she and the president were staying, and a special mattress was delivered to the hotel for the president's bad back. When John and Jackie awoke on the morning of November 22, thousands of people stood in the hotel parking lot chanting, "We want Kennedy!" After greeting the crowd, the couple left for Dallas.

Despite the generally very warm reception he had gotten so far, the president was somewhat worried about what Dallas would have in store for him. He said to Jackie, "You know, last night would have been a hell of a night to assassinate a president. I mean it. There was the rain, and the night, and we were all getting jostled. Suppose a man had a pistol in a briefcase? Then he could have dropped the gun and the briefcase, and melted away in the crowd.

Jackie, if someone wanted to shoot me from a window with a rifle, nobody can stop it. So why worry about it?"

November 22 was a lovely autumn day in Dallas, and President Kennedy received a warm greeting from more than 4,000 people at the airport. The president and Jackie smiled and waved as their limousine slowly made its way along overcrowded streets. Texas Governor John Connally and his wife sat in front of the president and Mrs. Kennedy.

The motorcade stopped several times at the president's request. He wanted to get close to the people, shake their hands, hear their voices. When he noticed a Catholic nun and her group of schoolchildren calling out to him, he ordered the motorcade to pause. Secret Service men, assigned the responsibility of protecting the president, quickly went to work, keeping the many well-wishers at a safe distance. Only the day before, hate posters were seen throughout the city, and that morning's *Dallas News* had run a full-page editorial criticizing President Kennedy's foreign policy. Though the crowd seemed friendly, the Secret Service was taking nearly every precaution to ensure the safety of the president.

One precaution the president had refused was the protective bubble shield that was normally placed over the presidential limousine. His advisers had urged him to reconsider and use the bubble, at least in Dallas. Jackie had even asked him to use it, veiling her concern for her husband's safety by pointing out that the bubble would keep her hair in place. Kennedy, however, wanted to be as close to the people as possible. The bubble would not be used.

Who would want to kill the president? A number of groups were considered potential threats. Many Cuban and Mexican Americans in Texas resented the Bay of Pigs fiasco. The Kennedy administration's crackdown on organized crime had angered many members of the Mob, and Southern racists were furious about Kennedy's support for the civil rights movement. Not only was Kennedy hated by the extreme right, but he was disliked by some moderate conservatives, who believed he was too willing to compromise with the Soviets. In addition, he was despised by left-wing radicals who believed he spent too much money on the military for fighting communism abroad.

At 12:30 P.M. that day, a man loaded a high-powered rifle on the sixth floor of the Texas School Book Depository building, the windows of which afforded a clear view of Dallas's Dealey Plaza, a scheduled passing point for the presidential motorcade. His name was Lee Harvey Oswald, and he was planning to kill the president.

As the motorcade proceeded down Main Street and approached Dealey Plaza, Mrs. Connally said, "Mr. President, you can't say Dallas doesn't love you." Seconds later shots rang out.

President Kennedy was hit twice, first in the throat and then in the head. Governor Connally was shot through the back, receiving injuries to his arm and leg as the bullet passed through his body. Jackie cried, "Oh, no, no . . . Oh, my God, they've shot my husband." She tried to climb over the back of the limousine, out of the assassin's range. A Secret Service man helped her back into the car, which immediately pulled out of the motorcade and rushed to Parkland Hospital.

The crowd at Dealy Plaza became frenzied. Many people were unsure of what had occurred. Some who heard the shots thought there had been a firing of cannons as a salute to the president. Others had seen the president collapse in his seat. Most people did not know if Kennedy had been hit once, twice, or at all. As the news was broadcast across the nation and around the globe, everyone feared the worst and hoped for the best.

President John F. Kennedy was pronounced dead at one o'clock that afternoon. Everything had been done to try to revive him, but the second bullet that struck the president had killed him. Mrs. Kennedy slipped her wedding ring on her husband's finger, and the white sheet was pulled up to cover his face. The body and the entire Kennedy entourage were transported back to Washington, D.C., on Air Force One. Kennedy had been the fourth United States president to be assassinated.

On the plane, Lyndon Baines Johnson was sworn in as the thirty-sixth president of the United States. This official act wasn't necessary — the United States Constitution provides that the vice-president immediately becomes president upon the death of his president — but Johnson believed that his being sworn in would reassure the country that in this time of crisis someone was in charge. As he took the oath of office, Jackie Kennedy stood beside him, her pink skirt still splattered with her husband's blood. She had decided not to change the skirt. "I want them to see what they've done to him," she told an aide.

The nation was shocked and overwhelmed with utter disbelief. In a few seconds, a great man, the leader of the free world, a husband, a father, had been brutally shot and killed. America felt as if it had been cheated, and it had been. An era of hope had ended abruptly, without reason or explanation. In a very real sense the brightness of America's future had been dimmed, and the nation's innocence had been lost. Ask anyone who was more than ten years old at the time of Kennedy's shooting where he or she was on that fateful day, and that person will be able to tell you.

A profound grief hung over the entire nation; America had never felt anything quite like the sudden loss of President Kennedy. The country began a period of mourning. Flags were flown at half mast, businesses were shut down, and schools were closed. Public places that were normally bustling were silent. People across the country and around the world were shocked into a state of dazed incredulity.

Americans stayed at home to be with their families and to watch the television coverage of the president's funeral at the Capitol rotunda, which was decorated, at Mrs. Kennedy's request, in the same way it had been for the funeral of President Lincoln, who was killed by an assassin's bullet in

1865. Television journalist Dan Rather described, twenty-five years later, how America felt in the fall of 1963: "There was a sense of John Kennedy, when he was alive, that wasn't the sense of greatness about him, it was the sense of potential greatness. Now that's pretty exciting, and it made the country exciting. John Kennedy, Mrs. Kennedy, and the whole Kennedy administration brought with them . . . excitement, energy, style, a sense of humor. So, when all of that ended in one terrible flash . . . this made the mourning all the deeper."

Europe also mourned the president's death. Prime Minister Harold Macmillan of Great Britain asked, "Why was this feeling — this sorrow — at once so universal and so individual? Was it not because he seemed, in his own person, to embody all the hopes and aspirations of this new world that is struggling to emerge?" In Copenhagen, Denmark, people surrounded the United States embassy with flowers. The people of West Berlin, a city that felt a unique loss at Kennedy's death, placed lit candles in the windows of their homes.

John Kennedy was buried in Virginia's Arlington National Cemetery, outside Washington D.C., on November 25, 1963. Leaders from nine-two countries attended the funeral, and millions of Americans paid their last respects to the late president. Jackie, whose strength and dignity helped carry the country through those difficult days, lit an eternal flame over her husband's grave, while their young children, John-John and Caroline, remained at her side. It was one of the saddest days in American history.

Lee Harvey Oswald was arrested at 2:15 P.M. the afternoon of the shooting and charged with the murder of President Kennedy. A former United States Marine and an outspoken Communist and Castro sympathizer, Oswald had lived for a time in the Soviet Union. There he met his wife, Marina, with whom he had two daughters. Oswald, whose father died before he was born, had had a very difficult childhood. He was raised by his mother, who moved from one Southern city to another, taking various odd jobs, trying to support herself and her young boy. To some of his acquaintances, Oswald seemed bitter about the hardship he knew as a child, and most people who met Oswald described him as a loner. Oswald never admitted killing the president, and after the shooting his mother said, "My boy couldn't have killed the president. I know him. Nobody else knows him. He's been persecuted so long."

Evidence linking Oswald to the murder weapon, which was found hidden in the Book Depository, was ample. He had gunpowder burns on his hands at the time of the arrest. His palm marks matched those on the rifle butt. He had ordered the rifle from a mail-order catalog. A photograph had turned up showing Oswald holding a rifle that looked identical to the rifle used to shoot the president.

It was likely that the Dallas County district attorney would call for the death penalty. Two days later, however, as Americans watched on national television, Oswald was shot as he was being transferred from the city jail to the county jail by Dallas police. His assassin, Jack Ruby, was a Dallas nightclub owner with alleged organized-crime connections. Oswald died in Parkland Hospital, the same hospital where the president had been pronounced dead only two days before.

Many questions remained surrounding the events of those few days. One of President Johnson's first acts in office was to create a commission headed by Earl Warren, chief justice of the Supreme Court, to conduct an investigation to answer as many questions as possible. Was the bullet that killed the president actually fired from Oswald's rifle? Or was there a co-assassin who was never caught? Some historians believe there is evidence to support either possibility. Did Oswald have a motive? Or was he simply a hired killer? Why did Jack Ruby kill Oswald? Did he simply want to punish Oswald for the crime himself? Or was he paid by someone who wanted to make sure Oswald did not reveal the names of others involved in the conspiracy? Ruby died of cancer in prison soon after his arrest for Oswald's murder. He never revealed his reasons for killing Oswald, perhaps fearing that if he named certain people as conspirators his family would be punished after he died.

The Warren Commission found that Oswald acted alone in killing the president, but many people continue to believe that the evidence strongly supports the conspiracy theory. Oswald's wife is among those who believe that Oswald acted as part of a conspiracy. Since the assassination, it has been alleged that the United States government has classified as top secret many documents that would clear up some of the mystery surrounding President Kennedy's assassination.

Reflecting on his brother's term in office, Bobby Kennedy said, "The essence of the Kennedy legacy is a willingness to try and to dare and to change, to hope . . . and risk the unknown." Thus, John Kennedy passed on to all Americans the determination to do better, the spirit, and the conviction that he himself inherited from his Irish immigrant ancestors.

Perhaps in some ways the Kennedy era has been romanticized, both by historians and by the people who lived during his time, believed in him, and saw him get struck down. Because of John Kennedy's tragic and senseless death at the young age of forty-six, the man has become a myth even when, after all, he was a man with faults as well as virtues. Kennedy's critics claim that he moved too slowly on domestic issues and was afraid to confront Congress on civil rights, yet when faced with violence and hatred in the South, he acted with moral dedication and toughness to usher in a new era of racial equality in America. While blamed for setting the stage for the United States' catastrophic involvement in Vietnam, Kennedy also fostered a distrust of military power as a means of achieving political ends and stirred the nation's conscience when he said, "The men who create power make an indispensable contribution to the nation's greatness. But the men who question power make a contribution just as indispensable, especially when that questioning is disinterested, for they determine whether we use power or power uses us. Our national strength matters. But the spirit which informs and controls our strength matters just as much."

Not even Kennedy's harshest critics could diminish the way he inspired the American people to believe that their concerted efforts could win the war against hatred and injustice. Tens of thousands of people, but especially the young, responded to his words "Ask what you can do for your country." Kennedy's charisma attracted the best and brightest people to work in government and touched the emotions of even the most skeptical observers to join in the struggle to create a better America. John Kennedy was carrying the torch for a new generation of Americans when their dreams were taken away by an assassin's bullet. Still, his legacy lives on.

What would life have been like in the United States if John F. Kennedy had lived to see his dreams become reality? Perhaps violin virtuoso Isaac Stern was right when he said of Kennedy, "I don't think we can ever romanticize what might have been had he lived. It would have been a glorious period in our history."

GLOSSARY

administration — literally, management. The administration of a government usually consists of a group of executives who are supposed to fulfill the government's duties. The word is also used to describe a government in general, as in "the Bush Administration."

adversary — an opponent in an argument, debate, or contest

aerial — of, relating to, or produced by the air; operating or operated overhead; relating to navigation: as in aerial navigation

allies — people or countries united by treaty, often to defend against aggression by others. In World War II, the United States, England, and France fought together against against Germany, Italy, and Japan and were known as the Allies.

annihilate — to destroy

blacklisted — a list of persons who are disapproved of or are to be punished or boycotted

blockade — to block or obstruct; a restrictive measure designed to obstruct the commerce and communications of an unfriendly nation

brainstorming — a group discussion characterized by a free flow of ideas and comments whose aim is to solve specific problems, gather information, stimulate creative thinking, and/or develop new ideas

capitalism — an economic system in which most of the industries and businesses in a country are owned privately, rather than by the government

civil disobedience — the refusal to obey certain governmental laws or demands for the purpose of influencing legislation or policy. Civil dis-obedience is generally performed by groups and is done without the use of violence.

Communist — a supporter of communism or member of the Communist Party. Communist societies are based upon the common ownership of property and are characterized by Communist Party control over all political and social activity and by central planning of the economy.

cooper — one who makes or repairs casks and/or barrels

debilitating — weakening

exiles — persons who are forcibly removed from their country or home

humanitarian — a person who promotes human welfare and social reform

imperialist — a person or nation who supports or practices imperialism. Imperialism is the policy by which one nation extends its rule or authority over another, often by force, but also by economic controls or cultural influence.

incriminating — something that shows proof of involvement with or responsibility for a crime or fault, as in incriminating evidence

inflation — a rise in prices. Inflation occurs when there is too much money and not enough goods available. It is caused by many factors, among them government spending levels, the practices of the business community, and international problems such as wars.

isolationist — a person or nation who supports or practices isolationism. Isolationism is a policy by which countries decline to enter into alliances and other political and economic relations with other countries.

liberalism — a political philosophy based on the belief in governmental guarantees of individual rights and civil liberties

maverick — an independent individual who does not go along with any group or party

moderation — the avoidance of extremes

nationalist — a supporter of nationalism, the belief that one's own nation is superior to all others; a member of a political party or group supporting national independence or strong national government

ousting — ejecting or removing someone from a place or position

racist — a person or state who practices racism. Racism is the belief that race is the primary element that determines human capabilities, and that a particular race produces superior or inferior peoples. Racists practice prejudice or discrimination based on race.

running mate — a candidate running for an office which is not the main office on the voting "ticket"; for example: the candidate for vice-president is the running mate of the presidential candidate.

scapegoat — one who is made to bear the blame for others, often without reason

segregation — the practice of maintaining separate facilities for members of different races, classes, sexes, ages, or ethnic groups

summit — in international relations, a meeting or conference of the highest-level officials (presidents, prime ministers) in a government

superpower — an extremely powerful nation; commonly used to describe the United States and the Soviet Union

Other books you might enjoy reading

1. Bishop, James A. *A Day in the Life of President Kennedy.* Random House, 1964.

2. Branch, Taylor. *Parting the Waters.* Simon & Schuster, 1988.

3. Cate, Curtis. *The Ideas of August: The Berlin Wall Crisis. 1961.* M. Evans, 1978.

4. Donovan, Robert J. *PT 109: John F. Kennedy in World War II.* McGraw-Hill, 1961.

5. Goldston, Robert. *The Coming of the Cold War.* Franklin Watts, 1977.

6. Levine, Israel E. *Young Man in the White House: John Fitzgerald Kennedy.* Messner, 1964.

7. Salinger, Pierre E. *With Kennedy.* Doubleday, 1966.

8. Schlesinger, Arthur M. *A Thousand Days: John F. Kennedy in the White House.* Houghton Mifflin, 1965.

9. Sorensen, Theodore C. *Kennedy.* Harper & Row, 1965.

10. Stirling, Dorothy. *Tear Down the Walls! A History of the American Civil Rights Movement.* Doubleday, 1968.

ABOUT THE AUTHOR

John W. Selfridge is an editor and free-lance writer with a special interest in twentieth-century history and culture. He received an M.A. in 1980 from Columbia University, where he studied literature and philosophy, and he is currently enrolled at Rutgers University Law School. An editor for a major New York City publishing house, he has been consulted on more than 100 young adult biographies.